The Art of Perfect Parenting

and Other Absurd Ideas

Andrew G. Yellen, Ph.D.
with the help of his wife,
parents and children

YELLEN & ASSOCIATES
Northridge, California

FIRST EDITION   November 1993

Book Design	Kate Cordoba
Proofreading	Charlayne Lacy
	Catherine Weinstein
Printing	Norsal Printing
Editors	Kate Cordoba
	Catherine Weinstein
Purchasing	Karma Kumar

Copyright © 1993 by Andrew G. Yellen, Ph.D.

Published by   Yellen & Associates
               11260 Wilbur Avenue, Suite 303
               Northridge, CA 91326
               (818) 360-3078

Library of Congress Cataloging-in-Publication Data

   Yellen Ph.D., Andrew G.
      Art of Perfect Parenting, The / Andrew G. Yellen,
      Ph.D.
      ISBN : 0-9639499-0-X : $10.95
      I. Title

Printed in the United States of America

WHY?

"Perfect parent" is a non sequitur. According to Webster's Dictionary, the definition of "non-sequitur" is "a statement that does not follow logically from the one that preceded it." The idea of a perfect parent certainly fits this definition to a tee. There is no such thing. On the other hand, we can get reasonably close with some degree of effort. Right now, as a whole society, we are not even close to being on target as effective parents. If we wish to reverse this trend, significant changes in parenting need to take place. Those who normally give advice on parenting tend to generalize. The advice needs to be far more specific. This book will leave you with a practical, highly effective means of imparting your values and priorities to the next generation in a very positive fashion.

Somewhere in the post World War II era we lost "it." That "it" refers to the ability to impart parenting skills to the next generation. There are many hypotheses as to why this occurred, but the signs are all there. Three out of five marriages end in divorce, and that number is increasing. Teen suicide has become epidemic. Drug use is crushing us. Crime has made it unsafe for most to venture out in many cases, and we have become prisoners in our own dwellings. Businesses say that today's young people are ill prepared to go out into the real world. Seemingly gone are the days when strolling on the beach at midnight was safe. People took pride in their accomplishments. Children cared about what happened beyond next week. The word "family" was an important part of everyone's vocabulary. Many would suggest that the single parent household changed things or that the two income family removed parental influence or that the media have become too powerful an influence. If that were the case, then how come there are still those families which manage to be successful and produce relatively healthy children who become relatively successful adults?

In my opinion the answers lay in parenting skills. Not to oversimplify, but I firmly believe that many of our societal ills could be effectively addressed by reestablishing parenting skills, empowering the parents to guide their children through to adulthood. Even much of the family therapy that is done is involved with restoring the parents to being the foundation of the children's behavior.

As the Introduction will explain, I was one of the fortunate few and as such feel a strong obligation. And I also live by the idea that I have to model appropriate behavior to our children. If I want them to turn things around, then I am responsible for starting the process. Sometimes I get the comment that my behavioral program is harsh, cruel, or unfair. Of course, this is usually made by parents who can't set any limits with their children either because of fear and guilt, lack of know-how, or a combination. What is really cruel is to turn an adolescent out into the big challenging world without the proper limits and skills necessary to survive. I'm sure I don't have to tell you. It really IS a mean, cruel world if you are not prepared. It's our job as parents to prepare our children.

To demonstrate that effective parenting is a learned skill that can be passed on, I've offered a three generational view. Hearing about parenting from three different perspectives insures you get a good look at a real life situation. Since my parents gave me the basis for my own parenting skills, they are the source. Their chapter is entitled "Directly From the Source." Our children are the results of these "experiments" and voice their comments in "The Next Generation." Besides, everyone is always asking my wife, Heidi, and me, "Yeah, what about your kids?" I asked both my parents and children to be very candid about what they wrote. For points of reference at the time of writing this book, my father was 78, my mother was 72, our son was 19, and our daughter was 15.

Of course, the other part of my personal philosophy is that most people take themselves too seriously. So, naturally, I can't do

Foreword

this whole thing with a perfectly straight face. I've always tried to mix practicality with a good sense humor. Usually a third of those I talk to think there's too much humor and I'm not serious enough, a third think I'm too practical and don't allow for emotions, and a third think I'm okay. I'm happy if those figures hold, since it seems to be a nice balance.

The book is divided into two parts. The first deals with parenting in general, the trials, tribulations, and anecdotes of an imperfect task. It is intended as a useful but light-hearted look at many of the factors that influence parenting in general. The second is a practical, hands on approach utilizing the Yellen Behavioral Management Program. This is the first book that goes beyond just simple advice and really integrates the many aspects of parenting into something that is useful on a consistent basis. It is designed to allow you to use the program almost immediately. It has been proven highly effective in many different family structures. It is not a panacea for everything that may occur in a family, but it will help you structure much of what you will need to accomplish with your children. My biggest wish is that all of this helps you with your parenting and that you enjoy your role as parent as much as Heidi and I have.

This book is dedicated to Ma and Pa Cookie.

TABLE OF CONTENTS

Part
I

TOOMUCH

PARENTINGMAKES

ONELOSEONE'S

MINDALTOGETHER

Chapter I - Introduction

No parent is perfect. I've always believed that my sister, Gay Denise, and I were extremely fortunate to have Ma and Pa Cookie for parents. We often heard from all of our friends how they would love to have them as parents. Actually, their names are Ruth and Al, but no one would recognize that anymore. Before going further, you are probably wondering how they got their nicknames?

My parents owned a bakery when our son, Josh, was about two and one-half years old. Once we were on the way to visit them with a friend. Every time we'd go to the bakery, my dad would give Josh a cookie. So, as we're driving, we asked Josh, "Wanna go see Pa?" His response was, "Cookie?" Our friend spouted, "Pa Cookie!" From that day forth, my parents were referred to by their friends, our friends, our family, our children's friends, our office staff, and probably half of the civilized world as "Ma and Pa Cookie."

Now, you have to understand that the following opinion is not only mine but is validated by everyone who knows them. They had an uncanny ability to do all the right things parents are supposed to do, and this was pointed out constantly by friends, relatives, and family members. Interestingly, however, my parents never pushed their ideas or made us feel as though they were always right. My parents were just there for us all the time. They parented by example.

Of course, as the title indicates, no parent is perfect. The following should serve to illustrate the point. I've always had a habit of getting out of bed in the middle of the night from the time I was able to walk to get a drink or go to the bathroom. Ma Cookie was told by her friends when I was about 6 years old that she needed to break me of this habit. Maybe they thought that children who grew up to be adults who got out of bed in the middle of the night turned into psychotic nocturnal weirdoes. So she listened to her girlfriends and warned me that if I got out of bed again, she would have a suitcase packed at the front door,

Introduction

and I would have to leave. Lo and behold, Mother Nature put me in a dilemma. Either I utilized my mattress as a urinal, or I tried to make it to the bathroom unnoticed. I got caught. So there I was, a little 6 year old, crying really hard, suitcase in hand, being escorted to the front door. Now, of course, my mother regrets the incident. She goes on about how foolish she was as a young mother and what an awful thing it was to do to a little one. So, even now, whenever she gives me a hard time, I ask, "Are you going to pack my suitcase and make me leave?" Even to this day, it gets her to feel guilty.

And then there was Pa Cookie's handling of my emergency situation as a little person, age 2, when we lived in New York. There were no walls or fences between houses or yards in those days. We more or less had one big community. Being the curious person that I was, I wandered over to a neighbor's and discovered what I thought was a bottle of apple juice. It turned out it was kerosene. Gagging and choking, I staggered home. My parents happened to be in the backyard. Seeing me in distress, then smelling the kerosene, Pa Cookie grabbed me, turned me upside down, and began trying to shake out the kerosene. This is not exactly the commonly practiced first-aid treatment recommended by the Red Cross. To this day, when I close my eyes, I can still see the ground coming at me with each shake. I was then taken to the emergency room and my stomach was pumped.

By now, you're thinking, "Great . . . just what I need . . . somebody's anecdotal life story." The purpose of explaining all of this to you is to illustrate that even the "creme de la creme" parents make errors. Rejoice! You are not alone. 99.9% of parents make parenting mistakes. The other .1% are liars.

So, Wonderful! Parents aren't perfect. Do we really need an entire book to say that? The answer is obviously "no." But we do need some insight into how to increase our win/loss ratio. What better way to start than to send everyone to the Ma and Pa Cookie School of Psychology, the good ole MPCSP. And this is no degree mill. You've got to work hard, and when you make an error (that's when, not if), you've got Ma and Pa Cookie there reminding you of what is correct and proper parenting.

Mothers of the world, celebrate! Not long ago, Ma Cookie and I disagreed on some point of parenting my children, Josh and Erit. In her opinion, I violated a classroom rule of parenting. In my efforts to allow the children to make their own decisions, I had placed them in a situation that they were not equipped to handle. The result was that both kids were very upset and felt guilty. I attempted to downplay the incident as merely a learning experience for them. My phone conversation went something like this: "Hi Mom." From the other end came, "I don't care if you're a doctor, I don't care if you're a psychologist, I don't care if you're the parent. I'm your mother and you're going to listen to me!" And of course I did.

At this point, any self-respecting psychotherapist is going to pronounce that my enmeshment with my parents is pathological, and that I have deep-seated, unresolved issues, particularly with my maternal progenitor. Maybe so, but I just happen to respect what many people consider a very valuable source of parenting information. If that's pathological, then lock me up and throw away the key.

This whole dissertation is designed to point up a very valuable lesson. We get our parenting skills from our parents. When we have had good role models and teachers, we then have good skills. But when something interferes with this process, such as divorce, latchkey, dysfunctionality of the family, or many other factors, we are not given an opportunity to learn good parenting skills.

All of this is compounded by a tremendous problem that will never change. Bear with me. I want you to imagine that you are in school preparing for a test. It is relayed to you that this test is one of the most significant you will ever take. Being the concerned person you are, you carefully organize your notes, you reevaluate your strategies, you spend considerable amounts of time, money, effort, on the latest, most up-to-date technological advances to help. You diligently go to study groups, you refrain from attending many social events, and, in general, you make tremendous sacrifices in hopes of really nailing down this test.

The big day arrives. As you enter the room, the air is thick with tension. All eyes are riveted on you. As you wander through the test, you realize that this is the hardest test you have ever taken. Beads of sweat begin to pour down your face. You check everything to the best of your ability. As you arise to turn in your paper, you are overtaken by a sinking feeling that you have no clear idea of the outcome. A phenomenal effort has been undertaken.

The professor collects all papers and then stands stoically in front of the class. "OK, class. The results will be available in 10 to 20 years. Class dismissed." You look and listen in horror, quickly doing a systematic check of all your senses to see if they're operating properly. To your dismay, every word was accurate. The depressed feeling is quickly overtaken by frustration, anger, and confusion.

Immediate feedback is mandatory for contentment in most learning experiences. Without the feedback we become uncertain about what to do next. All of us like to know how we're doing so we can continue along the same path, modify our actions, reject the whole package or shriek. The uncertainty breeds anxiety, panic, depression, and guilt. One begins to feel totally inadequate. If life ended after that all-important test with no real feedback, you would certainly complain. How could things get worse?

Welcome to parenthood! There are no specific guidelines, no rules, no coursework. It's probably the most important test of your life, AND you won't get the results for years. In most cases, by the time parents figure out what they might have changed, they're grandparents.

It's no small wonder that parents celebrate all the milestones in a child's life. Certainly parents might delude themselves into the belief that all the hoopla is for the child, but it is also self-validation that the parent has in some way been successful.

5

The Art of Perfect Parenting

There are many ways to attack an individual. But if one really wants to hurt someone, walk up to a person and, in a non-emotional, soft-spoken voice, state, "You know, I've been watching, and I have to tell you, I think you are a very incompetent parent." Better someone drive a stake through your heart. The pain would be much less.

The fact is that we, as parents, are constantly being "graded" by our peers. Basically, we have a "test" everyday. However, currently it appears that someone forgot to teach parents "how to study."

It's not really so much that values have changed. Parents still want respect, a good life, and happiness for their children. But somewhere along the way, we have lost the ability to impart these values to our children. I can't tell you how many times I've been asked, "Doctor, how badly have I messed up my child?" My response is, "I'm sorry. I don't do guilt. I have a whip in the closet, and you can go out to the parking lot and beat yourself up for 10 minutes. Other than that, you'll have to go somewhere else to get the guilt."

We need to be able to impart the good ideas to kids. So often I hear the overused excuse that societal influences are too strong to overcome. If that were the case, then how do these nay-sayers explain that many children grow up quite well and, in turn, become good parents? It is NOT by LUCK. Good parenting perpetuates good parenting. We've got to figure out what the key elements are for producing happy, emotionally healthy children — and the first place to start is by assessing what is normal. Welcome to your first subject at MPCSP (Ma & Pa Cookie School of Psychology).

Chapter II - "Hey Doc, Is My Child Normal?"

"How should I know? I'm a psychologist!" Surprised at the answer? Don't be. It's not that I don't consider myself a good parent. It's that people assume simply based upon my profession that my parenting will be phenomenal. Simply having the knowledge versus being able to impart that knowledge are two entirely different matters. A great athlete does not necessarily make a great coach. It is often the person who had to struggle to achieve who understands best how to educate.

Normal is in the eye of the beholder. Normal is DEFINITELY not what it used to be. Regardless of personal beliefs, single mother households are normal. Single father households are normal, gay and lesbian households are normal, both parents working households are normal, and, oh yes, husband-wife households are normal. They can be black, white, brown, yellow, red, or any combination. They can be rich, poor, or anything in between. Of course, each of these can also be abnormal. Who heads the household in this day and age does not determine normal.

Let me state right here, and I'll address the topic more completely in the chapter on behavioral management, that all the experts who claim to know exactly how children should be - values, priorities, and all - need to carefully reassess their function for those in their care or to whom they are dispensing information. The job of a parent should be to decide what he or she wants in children. The job of a therapist should be to provide the structure to implement the parent's ideas. As a parent, I would be quite offended if someone tried to tell me how my children should be, but I certainly would be willing to listen to a more effective way to put my ideas into action.

Books, television programs, seminars, and other resources are not the definitive source of what is normal. You could literally drive yourself nuts, if you haven't already, trying to figure out how your child should be. And furthermore, most of it has probably not worked. There are several good reasons.

The Art of Perfect Parenting

First, there is not such a thing as the generic family. This stereotype probably created as much walling off of differing individuals as any single idea. Everyone tried to be Hollywood's generic family, and everyone failed. Each family is its own entity with needs and priorities, some the same and some very different from other families. Hurrah for diversity. Life would be boring if everyone were the same. Oh, sure, this researcher says "this," and this researcher says, "that." Big deal. If everyone wanted to raise a statistic, they would go to mathematicians instead of therapists. We run into so much difficulty when we try to compartmentalize everyone.

I'd like to take a time out here to make a statement. I've probably offended some professionals by good-naturedly poking fun at a few of their antics. Intervening in such a delicate area as parenting is often a very difficult task. Especially when there are significant behavioral disorders, the therapist must keep the entire family system in mind while dealing with each individual's issues. Most professionals with which it has been my privilege to work do an incredible job of balancing all needs. I applaud the effort and work of those who have chosen to address such an important task.

Okay, back on track. A second reason that many of the behavioral programs have not worked is because they place people in the role of passive parents. "Okay, people, I'm the expert and if you follow steps 1 - 20 carefully (notice the similarity to a recipe), you will have the perfect child and you will be the perfect parent." Kinda like setting up a Ken and Barbie play-house, huh? I'm sure everyone has heard the old adage, "Give a person (updated to be non-sexist) a fish and he/she eats for a day. Teach him/her to fish and he/she eats for a lifetime." Well, along those lines, if we simply follow steps in parenting, we are limited to that particular set of circumstances, but if we set up a good structure by taking an active role in its foundations, we can handle many situations. Active parenting, in which the parents determine goals and ideas, is a far more effective method because everyone in the family has a vested interest of time, effort and love. Normal is what you as parents decide is normal. A great deal of the problem is tied up with the baby-boomer "open" style espoused in the 60's and early 70's. A child would walk up to an object, smash the object on the floor, and wait for a response. The parent response was, "My child has to learn to interact with his/her environment in an appropriate way." Interact, my foot! Where's the structure? Where's the limit setting? Assessing normal does not mean having no structure. The result is a generation that wouldn't recognize normal if it tripped over it, so how could this generation possibly be expected to impart "normalcy" to the next generation?

Firstly, define your objectives for your children. If you are unsure, consult various sources to help you, but do not look upon these sources as the only acceptable definition of normal. An expert is only someone who everyone else thinks knows what they are doing. Then, make sure you have an effective means of implementing your ideas. That's where good behavioral management comes in. It is not necessary to "reinvent the wheel" each time you wish to modify your child's behavior.

By this time, you're probably at the same point that many of the confused parents in my office have reached. Let me answer your question before you ask it. "Yes, but I won't." (Great! Now he's a mind reader.) The question is, "Can you give us specific examples of normal?" Don't get mad and throw the book in frustration. We're not going in circles. I hear you say, "But you just said I may not even know what is normal, and now you won't even give me an example so I know I'm on the right track!" The "what is normal" is really not significant at this time. It is a process of exploration for you, the parent. We don't get people in shape by doing the workouts for them. If parenting is a priority, and I will assume by virtue of the fact that you are reading this book that it is, then you're going to do the "workout." What is extremely significant is what you do once you have figured out what you want in your children. Again, I would never dare tell you how your children should be, but I certainly can provide you with some tools to implement your ideas.

What I can do is to give you the areas that you need to define. My suggestion is that you write out all your ideas so they become concrete rather than abstract. Parenting is a big job that requires much more work and energy than most people ever realize. Not to oversimplify, but in many ways, raising children is much like growing fruit trees. You must plant the seed, fertilize, water, pull weeds, hoe, turn over soil, trim unwanted branches, and provide a supportive environment all on a regular basis. When a disease or infestation occurs, you must treat it or the tree will wither and possibly die. You must protect it from creatures who would do it harm. When you're successful, you will have a beautiful tree that will grow strong and healthy and bear fruit. Neglect the tree, and the weeds take over. (Some gardening tips come with the package).

Write your own epitaph. "Excuse me?" you say. You read correctly. Write your own epitaph.

Now at this point you are seriously considering putting down the book. You've been shamed, guilted, confused, frustrated, and probably several other unpleasantries. You may have just begun to trust me, that possibly I was on to something when - BAM! - out comes that. Well, before you lock me up and throw away the key again, listen one moment.

If you really want to know what's significant in life, go to a funeral, go to a graveyard. You don't hear, "He was a wealthy man. She was a successful entrepreneur. He had the best grades in high school. She was a fine banker." What you see on gravestones and hear at funerals are values and priorities when people were successful. What would you like people to say when you're gone? This task is exceedingly difficult for most people because it forces us to deal with our own mortality. But if you're totally honest with your feelings, what better way to assess what's really important to you with such finality than to write your own epitaph?

In doing this, you will have identified what legacy you wish to pass on to the next generation. Why wait? Why not actively communicate that to your children rather than have them "realize" what you meant after you're gone? How many times have you heard others say years after someone has died, "I finally figured out what he/she meant." What a shame. Oh, but wait.

"Hey Doc, Is My Child Normal?"

Here come the therapists again. Obviously, according to theory, I'm secretly preoccupied with death, maybe I even have a death wish, to be so engrossed in a morbid thought, and I'm attempting to relay to the young parents that this is somehow okay. Right, and I wear a cape, have fangs, and suck blood, too!

So sit down and hammer out the details. What are the specifics of what you want to see in respect? What are the tenets of the parent-child relationship that you wish to establish? How would you like to have your child interact with others? What would indicate good self-esteem in your child? What are the values and priorities that you are unwilling to compromise on, and what are the areas in which your child is free to be an individual? What are the humanity values, the religious values, the cultural values, and the life skills that you wish to impart? What are the elements of yourself and your background that you wish to eliminate so that your mistakes of the past are not repeated?

Obviously, there is a considerable amount of work involved. (O.K., so I do a little guilt.) Isn't your child worth it? Someone once stated, "We never stand as tall as when we stoop to help a child."

Okay, folks. Remember that little train? "I think I can, I think I can." Normal is what you make it. That may be scary because now the ball is in your court. You are now responsible for the next generation and you're about to put what is normal in writing.

Yes, and for a nominal fee, you can rent Ma and Pa Cookie.

Chapter III - Is it Hopeless?

This chapter actually defies all the "correct" laws of writing an advice book. According to the pros, I'm supposed to lead you down this path of doom and gloom for the entire book. Then, just when you're about to jump out of a fourth story window in desperation . . . WHOOSH! I grab you in the final chapter. Well, I'm sorry, but I can't risk your doing something drastic by delaying help until the end. Besides, I'd much rather have you listening in a positive frame of mind. You're much more receptive with a smile on your face. Ma Cookie Lesson #58.

Nature vs. Nurture. This, of course, is an age old argument. Current research in psychology is quite clear that genetics plays a much greater role in personality than ever before realized. No, you can't punch out your boss and claim it was a genetic mutation that made you do it. You're still responsible. There is now no question that people have a genetic predisposition toward certain personality characteristics. In other words, many of the components of personality such as temperament, mood, and tolerance level are inherited. I tease our kids that they get to choose their own mates, but I get to choose their in-laws. Depression, anxiety, learning problems and many other factors have now been genetically linked. Wait! Before you go and get a gene transplant for your little darling, there's more.

You can influence your child in a very positive fashion. Of course, you can also influence your child in a very negative fashion. "Is it hopeless?" I hear you ask again. It's not hopeless, but there are some really serious qualifications. Beware! This could read like an insurance policy, complete with fine print and disclaimers.

One of the numerous ideas that my parents have taught me is that there is always hope. I've seen Ma and Pa Cookie take children who were acting up at a social function, birthday party or otherwise, and inside of one fifteen minute talk, drastically change the children's behavior, complete with smiles on the faces of most of the kids. Obviously, what Ma and Pa Cookie really needed to do was to give a similar talk to the parents. But always the diplomats, it was enough that the children behaved properly at that function.

Hopeless has too much finality to it to be ascribed to children. If hopeless were the case, then those in mental health should have their heads examined. As long as there are those who are willing to take the time and effort to address the issues of parenting, there will be hope. See, now don't you feel better? Now come the qualifiers.

Parents have to get out of their heads the idea that "there's nothing I can do." I'm not sure where many of today's parents get this belief, but I continuously sit with parents who feel powerless. How sad to say, "There is a seven (or whatever age) year old who runs my life." Rejoice!! There's a lot you can do to impact your child in very positive ways.

Imparting values at an early age will significantly help. In this modern, fast-pace age we often tend to overlook important life skill details. When we begin to evaluate "where things have gone wrong in society," the answer most often used as a common denominator is the lack of imparting important values to our children. It is, therefore, incumbent upon the parents to insure that proper values and priorities become part of the overall transgenerational process. This process can be divided into two steps.

Firstly, we, as parents, must specifically define what it is that we wish to pass on. Because of the great deterioration of generational communication, we most likely have clouded definitions of values and priorities. We need to take the time to sit down and actually write out what it is that we wish to pass on to our children. This allows us to externalize it, view it, modify it, embellish it, and perfect it so that we can truly focus on the transferring process.

Secondly, this transference needs to be both by cognitive structuring and by modeling. The expression, "Do as I say and not as I do" has no place in proper parenting. You need to discuss these values and priorities with your children on a regular basis, whether it be centered around a news event, a personal event, or a peer event. Not only does your child hear what you are saying, but her or his responses let you know how this information is being processed. However, the most important component of the transgenerational process is you. A child raised with love, learns to love, but a child raised with criticism learns to be critical. Which do you prefer be passed on as your legacy?

This information needs to be presented as a structured choice. Can you imagine opening the paper and seeing a headline that General Motors named a 10 year old as its president? Obviously, this would be a far-fetched headline, but understanding why is a very important aspect of parenting. The ten year old does not have either the cognitive ability or the decision-making and problem-solving skills necessary to successfully perform in this position. Somewhere between childhood and adulthood we assume our children will automatically "know" how to problem solve. We become quite upset when they cannot. Most parents fail to recognize that these are not instinctive skills but rather learned behaviors. The process should begin quite young and progress according to both the child's ability to make decisions and cognitive development. We, as parents, need to create structured choices.

A child of three, when asked the open-ended question, "What would you like for lunch?" may randomly reply, "Gummy bears and coke." The parent's response is "No, that's not a healthy lunch. What else would you like?" If the child responds inappropriately again, the same comment is given. Repeat this scenario hundreds of times, and your child "learns" he or she does not make good decisions. As a result, self-esteem declines, and your child ceases to make decisions on her or his own. This is not our objective.

However, give children a structured choice of, let's say, bologna or tuna sandwiches, and either choice is correct. When this scenario is repeated, your child is given the message that he or she makes good decisions. Self-esteem rises as confidence is gained, and as good problem-solving is practiced, your child becomes more proficient. As she or he is able, you expand the choices. At some point you can then ask the open-ended question, "What would you like for lunch?" The reply will likely be appropriate because responses have been structured. Help your child gain decision-making and problem-solving skills by structuring him or her for success.

One of the most significant influences on children is the modeling that is done by those held as most important to the child. Trying to justify behavior by saying that you are the adult and using that as the sole basis for the reason they should not imitate you is a set up for failure. To a child, weak is strong. Sound confusing? It is confusing to many parents, and they have difficulty with the issue.

To a fair percentage of parents the admission of a weakness or poor judgment to a child is withheld because of a fear of undermining the child's respect for the parent. Some parents feel that by presenting an aura of invincibility two things will occur. The child will feel much more secure, and discipline will be much easier. Both of these beliefs are flawed.

Initially, the child may feel secure and place the parent high on a pedestal. No one is errorless, and children of all ages to some degree can sense when something is not correct, regardless of what they are being told. When (that's "when" not "if") the child discovers the "perfect" parent has made an error, the results can be devastating. A very unrealistic, idealized image is shattered leaving the child extremely insecure.

At the same time, feeling cheated and lied to, discipline with the child becomes quite difficult. He or she develops anger that may get acted out against the parent. It may be in either an active or passive fashion, but the child will retaliate.

But perhaps of even greater significance is the fact that you are your child's favorite role model. While he or she may still be angry, this type of parenting behavior, the denial of errors, will become part of his or her own skills.

The Art of Perfect Parenting

When a parent can admit vulnerability and take the necessary steps to correct or compensate, three vital things are accomplished. Firstly, the child develops a realistic and healthy perception of parents. Secondly, discipline is actually easier because the child can relate to admission of error without shame and realizes that addressing a weakness, not covering up, is preferred. Thirdly, you, as the most important figure for your child, have successfully modeled proper accountability for behavior.

I'm reminded of an incident from my childhood that is imprinted in my mind forever. Growing up we were wealthy, but we did not have a lot of money or luxuries. No, this is not a contradiction. We had something that no one could take away. We had us. But money was a short commodity. So one day when Pa Cookie came home with a bank bag loaded with about three times his annual salary, our faces lit up. He had found the bag on the ground at the bank when he had gone to make a nightly deposit. When we began to jump for joy, he immediately stopped us. The money was not ours, and he was taking it back in the morning when the bank opened. Other than when I'm sleeping, it was one of the few times in my life that I was silent. No lectures on right versus wrong. No long drawn-out, anecdotal fables. Just an action, but, boy, did that action have an impact. When my son was about twelve years old, he and I had gone to the college library to do some research. In the parking lot, I discovered a wallet containing about $60. My son looked at me and waited. I handed him the wallet without a word. After about 30 seconds, I asked him to see if there was any identification. After finding the identification, I asked him what he thought would be a good idea. He shrugged his shoulders. I pointed to a campus police officer who was in the parking lot, and we walked over to him. Josh looked up at me, and handed the officer the wallet. As we walked to the library he just smiled. No lectures on right versus wrong. No long drawn-out, anecdotal fables. Just an action, but, boy, did that action have an impact.

You must also provide an accurate reflection for your child. The Talmud, which is a Hebrew book explaining what is meant in the

Is it Hopeless?

Bible through stories and fables, describes two men with the occupation of chimney sweep. After a very difficult job, both men emerge from the top of the chimney to rest. Each is facing the other. One man's face is completely covered with soot, while the other's is completely clean. According to the story, one man leaves to wash his face while the other remains. The question posed is, "Which man goes to wash his face and why?"

Many answer that obviously the man with the dirty face goes to wash away all the soot. Scholars suggest that this simplified answer is given impulsively with little thought given to social interaction or social modeling. An examination of the "deeper" meaning is in order.

Each of us is dependent upon others in our environment to validate our own actions and reactions, thoughts, and emotions. Others act as a mirror. When this mirror is polished and clear, we receive an accurate, undistorted view of ourselves. If not, we cannot get a reliable picture.

Each of us can only react to what he or she believes to be real. Our actions and reactions, feelings, and emotions will be based upon what reflections we see. As an example, even after looking in a mirror when donning a new outfit, many of us still seek the emotional support of a reliable individual by asking, "How do I look?" The more secure we are, the more we trust our own senses. But the more insecure we are, the more we need to double and triple check because we do not trust ourselves. "How do I look? Are you sure? Would I look better in something else?"

Your child needs an accurate mirror, not one that only selectively reports reality or one that has its own agenda. As the parent, you help establish security by being nurturing and by validating actions and reactions, feelings, and emotions. You see, the man with the clean face looked at his colleague's soot-laden face and left to wash his own.

Another ray of hope is rooted in teaching children to go pan for gold. Hold on a moment, I'm not off the wall. Teach your child how to collect "nuggets." Did I hear someone ask what I mean by nuggets? Please allow me to explain. Our children often ask where I got information on such a broad number of topics. Of course, because they are between 12 and 22, I have lost my intelligence, and they are perplexed about how I've survived this long without their guidance. Oh, don't worry. All parents lose their intelligence when their children turn about 12 and then miraculously regain it when the children turn about 22. Isn't it a coincidence how our intelligence returns at the same time the children complete much of their own education? So maybe they ask just as a courtesy. But it makes me feel useful anyway.

When you pan for gold, you have to sift through tons of gravel just to get a nugget. The miner who is persistent and continues to sift through debris winds up with a stack of nuggets worth a fortune. This is not so dissimilar from "nuggets" of knowledge. Now, you know you can't just hand these nuggets to your kids. That's called a set up for instant rejection. You strategically have to leave the nuggets in your children's paths and act totally surprised when they find the nuggets. Nothing will have a better impact on the kids than thinking they've discovered all the secrets of the meaning to life on their own. Just sit back and smile, knowing that you are structuring success.

Nuggets can be anywhere and everywhere and from anyone. If you are receptive, the sources are limitless . . . IF you are receptive. I learned a great lesson a long time ago that helped me realize that "nuggets" could be found from some of the most unlikely sources.

I was never a car nut as a kid, but I was pretty mechanical. One Saturday, when I was 15, a friend had asked me for some help with an engine. We had to remove four big bolts. Three came loose easily, but, of course, Murphy showed up (whatever can go wrong, will go wrong). So there we were, two youths, trying all we knew about levers and mechanical ingenuity, stumped. We were sitting on the curb, very tired, swearing at the bolt (somehow people are convinced that if you swear at inanimate objects, they'll perform better). Out of nowhere comes an elderly gentleman. He was walking slowly and appeared disheveled. "Hi boys. Whatya doin'?" he inquired. We calmly, but quite condescendingly, explained that we were trying to get a bolt loose. "Mind if I try?" he asked. We looked at each other and thought, "Yeah. Right! Here's the two of us, strong and knowledgeable, not being able to do it. And he thinks he's got a shot? Hah, hah." Not to be rude, we agreed to let him try.

We were convinced that this man was from another planet when he positioned himself seated on the street, facing the passenger front door, legs under the car, with his lower back against the curb. He then asked us to go over to the other side, reach under the car, put the wrench on the bolt, put a pipe on the wrench, and put his left foot on the pipe. He proceeded to place his right foot on the pipe also. After a mild grunt, he stood up, walked about ten feet away and turned to us. Staring in shock we listened to him matter-of-factly say, "Boys, don't ever forget that your legs are stronger than your arms."

This may not seem like an event that would determine the fate of the planet, but it did have a significant impact on me. Had I, for whatever reason, opted not to allow the scenario to develop, I would have missed the lesson. Always listen, then evaluate. I can always choose to ignore the information, but I can't always find information. So there we stood, awestruck and dumbfounded, while this elderly man walked away.

This lesson was reinforced in a number of different ways and different perspectives over the years. The first was about a year later as a senior in high school. I was on the track team in the spring semester as a shotputter. The local YMCA had asked our school and my coach to use the school's facilities for their track meet on a Saturday. Coach said "yes" and also volunteered a number of us to help. Please note I'm an ex-college athlete and a former coach. When your coach says, "Jump!" you ask how high on your way up. So my early Saturday morning was spent helping get the track facilities prepared. Because land was at a premium, Los Angeles City Schools did not have enough room to include the discus event in a safe fashion. But because there were only my coach and a couple of teammates there, Coach brought us over and showed us the spin technique for the discus, and we threw it to an empty field. Basically, the discus is held at arm's length, and the athlete rotates rapidly about two times, releasing the build up of centrifugal force. Please be patient with me a moment, and you'll understand why I'm explaining discus technique in a parenting book. We all went back to work getting the shot put area ready. But the curiosity bug bit me. I reasoned that if centrifugal force worked for the discus, why couldn't the same laws of physics be applied to the shot put? At that point in time the shot put was more or less a "slide across the ring, turn, and heave it as far as you can" technique. So I experimented (I can actually blame this on Ma and Pa Cookie for teaching me to be a critical thinker and not settle for the status quo). To my delight it worked! Within two or three tries that shot was taking off like a cannon ball. "Coach, Coach!"

Okay, now here comes that lesson from a different perspective. His response was, "Yellen, just stick to what I taught you. You know nothing about kinesiology, and it won't work." So, of course, I forgot about it, because my coach said so.

Lo and behold! Several years later appeared the sports' headline "Brian Oldfeld Sets New World Record Mark in Shot Put with New Technique." Guess what technique he was using, folks. You bet, it was the same technique that a brash 17 year old had once tried. I immediately called my old coach and jabbed that the technique could have been named after him, if he had only bothered to listen. We were friends, so he just laughed and agreed that I was absolutely correct.

The point here, again, is that nuggets can come from anywhere. If you are not constantly open and receptive, you'll miss 'em. And now for the practical application side of the lesson.

In my other life I was a head football and swimming coach. My team was in a critical situation during a playoff game, when I called a time out. I had the headphones on getting information from the press box, my assistant coach was giving me his opinion, and I gave my quarterback (QB) the play. My QB said, "Coach, I saw something out there I think would work." He was promptly told by everyone around us, including the principal, to shut up and run the play. Something in the back of my head said "nuggets." I told everyone else to be quiet and get away. I asked my QB what he saw. He told me that twice earlier in the game when this particular opponent was put in, the other team ran a certain defensive coverage that left one of our receivers wide open. The call defied what most armchair quarterbacks would have done, but . . . after his idea became a 68 yard touchdown pass, no one asked anymore questions or gave any unsolicited criticisms.

Listening skills are a critical component of parenting. It is exceedingly important that parents listen to what is being said AND to what is NOT being said. When a situation is distasteful or painful, children have a tendency to do one of two things. Either they will talk it to death or will make the thoughts disappear. How often after a tragedy have you heard parents say, "If only I would have listened to her/him?" Be an active listener by listening carefully to what is being communicated, not only in words but in body language and moods. Don't try to oversimplify the problem. While it may not be a significant issue to you, it may hold much importance for the child. Some of the communication may be noteworthy and some not. As a concerned parent, you'll have to sift through all of it. On the other hand, if your child tries to push those thoughts away, the thoughts may be eliminated during conversations. Not having a child mention something that should be part of a "big picture" is certainly worth pursuing. It may only be an oversight, but it may also be very significant. If there are serious issues, they may be masked and distorted to the point of being unrecognizable. At that point, no one knows where that may lead. A comparable situation would be a wet spot in your ceiling. You can see the water spot because it is the end result. But the leak in the roof that started the process may be on the other side of the house, and the water traveled along one of the rafters. It is far easier to identify the leak in the first place than to try to trace it back from the wet spot in the ceiling. Similarly, identifying your child's problem at the source allows you to address the problem area immediately, rather than having it surface in another manner. Listening carefully and then confronting the issues in a supportive manner prevents your child from covering up matters that need to be addressed.

But perhaps of all the influences on a child, nothing will have more impact than "No Strings Love." Nothing creates better self esteem or a psychologically healthier person than "No Strings Love." Conversely, few things can destroy a person faster than having love attached to some type of performance.

When children are loved with no strings attached, meaning they do not have to be a certain way, or do something in a certain way in order to be loved, they grow up with a great sense of security and a stable foundation. They are self confident because their foundation is always with them. Children given such love also develop into adults who can offer this gift to others, whether as a partner or as a parent. The children are happier and more content since they are free to be themselves, and yet have been structured enough to use this freedom wisely.

But when we attach our love and affection to performance, we create individuals who are not free to express or be themselves because they live in constant fear of rejection. The effects of rejection at any age, but particularly on a child, are devastating. These children grow up constantly trying to please everyone in their environment. Even when they can please one person, that success will be discounted. Continuously seeking out others for validation, they will always live in constant fear of rejection and abandonment.

No one is suggesting that a child be allowed to do or say anything he or she pleases. All children need and want struc-tured choices. But to attach love to performance is to undermine healthy development. Rewards and consequences are appropri-ate for behaviors and are a part of life. Love should be used generously as a reward, but the withholding of love should NEVER be utilized as a consequence.

At this point hopefully the question "Is It Hopeless?" has been thoroughly addressed. Remember that disclaimer? IF you put in the time, energy, and effort, it is far from hopeless.

Chapter IV - Discarding Your Own Garbage

If there is one thing that I've learned over the years, it's how good a job adults do of screwing up kids. Now, don't get me wrong. Most of the time it is definitely not intentional. We just simply keep "tradition" going. What we first have to do is identify those characteristics within ourselves that need to be modified or deleted, otherwise we just perpetuate the bags of garbage.

Children often give away that they have done something inappropriate. Parents will say that the child "looks" guilty. In reality what the parent is actually sensing is the effort, verbal and nonverbal, to cover up a secret. Most young children are not masterful at the deception. However, as they grow older, many children become extremely skillful at keeping secrets. In most of these cases they have had excellent teachers and role models to learn from . . . their parents.

The level of dysfunctionality in an individual, family, or system can almost be tangibly measured by the number of secrets kept. As an example, the most secretive families are those in which abuse or molestation have taken place. The system makes every effort to insure that no information gets out or in, hence a closed system. All parties are cut off and isolated to avoid "comparing notes." By contrast, the healthiest of individuals or systems encourage open communication. No one fears that "secrets" may leak. Problems are confronted.

The emotional effort and energy required to keep the secret can be devastating. At the very least it has a detrimental effect on a child's future relationships because the need to keep secrets gets passed on from generation to generation as a destructive force.

Is there a level of dysfunctionality in your family? Do you promote open and honest communication or do you cultivate secrets? Remember that just words alone are not sufficient. Words must be backed by appropriate actions.

The Art of Perfect Parenting

You also need to recognize the "skeletons in your closet" that trigger off unexplained emotional responses in you. Have you ever been listening to or watching a person or people only to unexpectedly feel as though you have just been punched in the stomach, suffocated, ready to faint, or otherwise violated? You glance around to observe if there are others reacting in the same fashion to what was heard or seen only to find that no one else gave it a second thought.

You are not alone. Each of us has triggers from the past, skeletons that are hidden beneath many years of denial, compensation, or possibly repression. These triggers produce a cascade of emotional reactions, some turning to physical responses. They are long established habits tied to years of patterned reactions, probably from early childhood. Not all are negative. The words or actions of others often elicit warm feelings or memories.

Your child may unwittingly pull one of your negative emotional triggers, causing you to overreact to an event. It is important that you be aware of these hidden skeletons.

Your overreaction, without an age-appropriate explanation to your child, will give him/her an incorrect message. The child will believe he or she has done something to warrant such an intense reaction. Feelings of shame and guilt will arise in response to something that should have been handled relatively easily.

It's imperative that children not be loaded with "excess garbage." Left unaddressed, your issues will become part of the transgenerational package that we, as parents, often pass on. Take the time to recognize where your feelings are rooted. You may not be able to stop your own reactions, but your child should not be an innocent victim of your past.

So often we focus only on what is wrong. How many of us heard, "So you got 3 A's, 2 B's, and a C. How come you got the C?" Fortunately, I was one of the lucky people who never heard those kind of remarks. We have to drop the idea that anyone is going to be perfect. As individuals, some of the best advice to be listened to is, "Don't let what you can't do interfere with what you can do." Frequently people are so focused on difficulties they neglect to explore and strengthen those qualities that will lead to success. As parents, it is most important that we impart positive beliefs to our children.

Children take their cues from other people in their environment whom they perceive to be significant. The primary people for most children are parents but can include extended family, teachers, rabbis, ministers, and other authority figures. When those in the child's environment focus on negative issues about the child, such as disorders, disabilities, or behavior, self esteem deteriorates and positive qualities about the child begin to be discounted, not only by the parent but by the child herself/himself.

Evaluate your communication with your child on a daily basis. Examine what percentage of that communication focuses on some negative aspect and interrogation. What we tend to do is to expect that things will go well without any positive reinforcement, reward, or praise but we punish offending actions. How often have we heard, "The child should do it because it is correct and has its own reward?" But we are so quick to address the behavior if it is not present.

Many of us need to change the ratio of positive communication to negative communication. Even with difficult, hard to manage behavior, the ratio should remain at least 50-50. No child does everything wrong every day. Whether it is politeness, helping, or even simply not having any inappropriate behavior, let your child know that you are aware. Set a goal of a ratio of 75-80 % positive to 20-25% negative. Check yourself on a regular basis. Your child's positive response and rise in self esteem will be reflected in all environments in which he/she has contact. As the parent, you are certainly the key component of positive behavior.

How many times do you remember hearing things such as, "He didn't really mean that," or "You know she really loves you?"

The Art of Perfect Parenting

How many times have you made similar statements to your child? These comments have hidden and confusing messages that you may not wish to convey.

As an example, let's assume that one parent has become frustrated and exasperated from continuous conflict with a child. That parent loses control and does something that he or she later regrets. In the meantime, the other parent, sensing that the child is upset and that the inappropriate action by the first parent was one of impulsivity and not intentional, tries to cover up the action with the explanation that the offending parent really does care about the child. The logic of the adult mind accepts that the two can exist at the same time.

However, the hidden message to the child is that, somehow, this inappropriate, hurtful action is to be interpreted as love. If the scenario is repeated, the child develops with the belief that the offending parent's inappropriate behavior is to be included in the child's reflections of love. And this behavior will certainly be passed on.

The real question - Is That Really the Message You Want to Give?

Chapter V - Adultisms vs. Ego Boosters

Adultisms–there is no other term that fits. Adultisms are those negative terms, phrases, or ideas that seem to be part of parent/ adult audio tapes of the mind that get replayed to the next generation simply because we once heard them. They are born out of frustration, anger, and loss of control on the part of the parent. They serve no constructive purpose and only serve to undermine children's self esteem. Buried somewhere in our mature minds is a tape recorder that keeps on looping. Sometimes it surprises us so much that we actually make statements like, "I'm beginning to sound just like my mother (father)!" Successful parenting requires that we exorcise these from our being so they do not interfere in our effectiveness. But first, let's identify some of these little gems. Feel free to jump right in and fill in the ends of the sentences with whatever you are currently telling your child. The following is only a sampling. I'm sure each of you has your own memory of a phrase that made you feel like vomiting. For clarification I've divided these adultisms into four convenient groups: Questions; Shoulds; Facts; Ifs.

The Questions

How come you never . . . This is wonderful indication that in all the years of your child's existence he or she NEVER did whatever it is that you are criticizing. Of course, your logical mind, when confronted in an unemotional fashion, will readily admit that there are times your child does what is correct, but, hey, you were upset.

Why can't you ever . . . A hybrid of dig number one, this not only indicates that your child "never," but that he or she is incapable FOREVER. What a wonderful ego booster.

Why do you always . . . This meaningful phrase is the exact opposite of the first one. You basically are indicating that your child does the same inappropriate action 100% of the time with no exceptions. No one does something ALWAYS, least of

27

all children, but they'll begin to believe you.

Where are your brains? This is a full frontal attack with no subtleties. Did you expect your child to go looking for his or her brains and bring them back in answer to your question? The "understood" portion of this statement is that the child has no brains at the current time.

Where did you come from? Once, again, the frontal attack. From the child's point of view, she or he has just been excommunicated from the family. The meaning is clear– somehow they don't belong because of some particular action. Gee! Why does my child feel isolated?

Where were you raised? Unlike the previous, at least the child can believe they come from this planet. However, you've just denied their reality because they always thought they were raised with you.

How many times have . . . Did you want your child to keep a log of your statements or perhaps receive a math grade for addition? What would you do if they actually gave you a number?

When will you grow up? They're children! They'll grow up when they are supposed to. Of course, they will grow up a lot healthier without comments or questions like this one.

Do you want to grow up to be . . . Great! First you question whether they are going to grow up at all, and then you scare the hell out of them that they are growing up. What if they grew up to be YOU?

Why can't you be like . . . Children need to be themselves and not be compared to other kids. This question completely invalidates the child as a person. It basically states they have no merit on their own.

What do you have to be sad about? The problem is that if they actually answer, you have a tendency to even put them down for the answer. So there stands the little person who's condemned for answering or not answering. Great choice.

What made you think ... In other words, how dare you think since you obviously don't have the tools to make a proper decision.

O.K. But how come you didn't ... This represents the old classic that nothing the child does is ever good enough. They spend the rest of their lives trying to attain perfection, all the while believing they are failures if they don't.

The Shoulds

You should know better. Well, let's ask this question. Did you teach them to know better or just assume they would get it by osmosis?

You should be ashamed of . . . This is especially effective at crushing self esteem when the word "yourself" is inserted. Shame and blame are the foundations of codependency and dysfunction.

You shouldn't feel ... This is the root of many problems as an adult. In essence, what happens is that a child ties a body response or sense to a particular event but is then told this "feeling" is incorrect. The result is free floating anxiety. All people, yes, even children, are allowed to have their feelings without having to justify, explain, or become defensive.

The Facts

You never appreciate ... There's that word again—never. Now, let's be realistic. Is it really a fact that your child NEVER appreciates you? And furthermore, do you model appreciation for your child?

You don't feel . . . This is simply a more emphatic form of the "should" version. Flat out, kid, your feelings are not correct.

There's nothing to be afraid of. This is just a more specific declaration of the previous fact.

You're just lucky that . . . This lovely idea leads to the belief that at any moment the entire world may come crashing down upon the child, that only by luck have they evaded the inevitable. Does the word "neurotic" apply?

Someday you'll . . . Hey, nice work. At least there's hope. The child might achieve "someday" (probably if they're perfect).

You're not really in love with . . . This is a great one for making a teenager really angry. It not only totally discounts age appropriate feelings that they might have, but really screws them up in the relationship, as well.

You don't really hate . . . The opposite of the last one, again, totally discounts individual feelings. If you would like to discuss strong feelings and emotions with your child, please do so in a non-judgmental fashion.

You don't really think . . . Along the same lines as the two previous comments, the child is not only denied of feelings, but now thoughts as well. The hidden message is that they really have no mind at all.

The Ifs

This category is actually a quite sophisticated one. There is a cause and effect relationship established between the child's behavior and the happiness of the parent, thereby placing the burden squarely on the child's shoulders.

If you really loved me, you would . . . Wow! Project this one forward several years, and you've produced a codependent adult who attempts to jump through hoops on every occasion just to avoid rejection. Talk about doing a guilt trip on someone.

Adultisms vs. Ego Boosters

If you really cared . . . This is just a watered down version of the previous comment, but basically designed to accomplish the same thing.

If I were you . . . Usually this is a comment to a completely unsolicited question. If you are asked, that's one thing. You are not your child, so don't pretend to be.

If only you would have . . . This is a set up. Basically, the theme here is "Pick A or B. Oh, you picked A–sorry that's wrong. You picked B–sorry that's wrong, too." Trial and error is a powerful teacher, and children need the freedom to risk error without feeling shame.

Ego Boosters, on the other hand, make kids, and really all people, feel good about themselves and the decisions they have made. They are an important component in producing healthy, self assured, critical thinking, sensitive individuals who are not only confident in facing the challenges that await them but have the skills necessary to be successful most of the time. A few of these comments well-placed will prove fantastic.

That's interesting. Tell me about it. This is a great substitute for "What's that?" because you are not giving the message that somehow they haven't accurately represented reality.

It sounds like you might be feeling . . . When you're ready, I'd like to hear about it. Not only are you validating and showing respect for feelings but you are showing interest, as well.

It seems like that's difficult. When you're ready, I'd like to help. Here you are acknowledging a child's difficulty, letting them have their space, and offering to help rather than just criticize.

I was wrong. I'd like to apologize. Wow! What a novel idea. This is an adult admission of making an error and not becoming defensive or denying.

I really like the way you . . . Purely and simply a compliment with no strings attached. See how many of this type you can perform each day.

You decide. You make great decisions. And then you must support that decision.

Or, just because, throw in a bunch of these: Wow!; Way to go; Super; You're special; Outstanding; Excellent; Well done; Remarkable; Awesome; You made my day; Terrific; Phenomenal; Sensational; Superb; I love being with you; You're incredible; Fantastic; Dynamite; Unique; What a winner; Magnificent, Marvelous; I admire you; I respect you; You make me laugh; You brighten my day; I'm impressed.

How many times a day do you use these instead of the adultisms? It's really a lot easier than you think. The excuse I most often hear is that the kids don't do that much that is positive. This is a process, and the first step is to be made by you. FIND the positive things your child does, no matter how insignificant those things may seem.

Chapter VI - The Modern Age

For many parents the idea of "going out" conjures up images of one boy and one girl or double, even triple dating. The immediate assumption was that everyone was paired up. To have an odd number of people or other than a 50-50 ratio meant that someone in the group was without a date and simply tagging along.

Enter the modern adolescent era. It is quite common and socially acceptable by teenagers to go out as a group. Actually, in most instances the gender ratio is not balanced. There exists much more of a group mentality than what was previously accepted. Prior generations felt very uncomfortable if that ratio was unbalanced, particularly when it was higher for males-obviously an expression of the double standard.

This group approach is reflected in art forms, music, dance, and particularly in clothing and has been adopted by younger generations. Many parents are uncomfortable with and unwilling to accept the idea of two or three females and five or six males, or the reverse, going out together with no intentions of "pairing off." The adolescents think of many of their parents' views as "perverted," as one such teenager so pointedly stated. Today's teens genuinely do not understand why a group, regardless of its composition, can not simply "hang out together." To quote Bob Dylan, "Oh, the times, they are a changin'."

Remember the movie "Weird Science" in which two adolescent males create the perfect female of their dreams via a computer? They seemed quite comfortable working on such a strange project, pecking away at a keyboard. To many a parent, the idea was not even comprehensible. This simple but poignant example highlights the essence of both generational jealousy and admiration with regard to modern technologies.

It was not too long ago that having a transistor radio that could be carried anywhere was a "far out" idea to most adults. Prior to that, having a television in a house was a luxury. We have progressed to the point that consumer electronics is a major factor in world economics. Are these items simply more complex toys, better learning tools, or a combination of both?

The answer lies in the manner in which the gadgets are used. If their use is not structured, then they simply remain as games. However, when they are put in the context of an educational tool, the learning process is greatly enhanced by becoming more interesting and efficient. Especially to the child with learning difficulties, these aids allow for a variety of compensatory strategies that were not possible a number of years ago. Even the dreaded "Nintendo" provides work on visual pursuit, simultaneous processing, anticipatory strategies, and many other subtle skills.

What becomes frustrating is having to ask your child for assistance with electronic paraphernalia because of both phobia and lack of knowledge. We are jealous that today's students have access to what would have saved us hundreds of hours in time and effort.

An electronic organizer, computer, spell checker, modem, and sophisticated telephone are but a few of the tools to benefit your child and make her or him more productive and marketable after completion of school. Step into the electronic generation and enjoy.

S & D - That stands for sex and drugs. It is your responsibility and obligation to discuss these with your child. If you don't, someone else will, but maybe not with the same information and feelings that you would prefer. So many parents are afraid to broach these subjects, opting instead to wait for schools or whatever. The results can be painful, even tragic. Now I realize that I'm walking on some touchy areas religiously, morally, and philosophically, but remember that the parents still decide what is correct for the family. As a society we are expected to all be great lovers as if this is some genetic coding that gets passed on. And, of course, we all know that men are supposed to "sow their wild oats" and have as many sexual conquests as possible, but females are to remain virginal until matrimony. There must be a lot of scared sheep in the barnyard when the boys come around. Such beliefs do nothing but perpetuate gender related stereotypes and confusion between and among men and women. Without stirring the wrath of the various gender movements, suffice it to say that men AND women contribute to many of the conflicts and misperceptions surrounding sex and intimacy.

When our son was in the third grade, he came home one day and said, "Dad, Kevin's lucky. He has an older brother." I replied, "Oh, and why's that?" He blurted back, "Because he gets to see his brother's Playboy." I suggested that he could have one, too. We were going out to dinner that night, so I told him we could stop after dinner. We first ventured into a major chain drug store. I told Josh that he'd have to go ask himself. Rather shyly, he approached the clerk and asked if the store carried Playboy. The clerk shot a glance at me, and I nodded in approval. The clerk indicated that they did not carry the magazine but suggested a liquor store. Josh's comment was, " That wasn't so bad, Dad." We went about two blocks to a local liquor store. As we entered, there were about ten people in the store. Josh proudly inquired from about 20 feet away from the counter in a rather loud voice, "Excuse me, sir. You carry Playboy?" After glancing at me for an okay, the clerk directed him to the rack. But now Josh was faced with another problem. His world of taboo magazines just got significantly bigger. He wanted to know why several of them were wrapped in cellophane. Of course, that became the forbidden fruit. When he asked if he could get one of those, I said yes. For three solid hours at home he glared at the magazine and then more the next morning. He then proclaimed, "This is disgusting!" We had a great, age-appropriate talk about intimacy, caring, and physical affection. Rather than feeling shame, he now feels sensitivity and affection. And in case you're wondering, we do not have a double standard. Our daughter has received the same information regarding sex, reproduction, and love. Many parents are embarrassed and ashamed to discuss sex and intimacy because that's the way they were raised. In addition, many youths actually do have more knowledge about the subject than parents. Parents need to educate themselves first in many cases. Maybe then a parent won't ask the ignorant question that was asked of one of my teenage female patients. She was asked by her parent–How did that happen? Having strong values does not mean avoiding issues that desperately need discussion. In this era of HIV and AIDS nothing as important as your child's life should be left to chance. Having children does not make you an expert on sex and reproduction. You need to be able to give your children proper answers or direct them to an appropriate source. Another important component of the sex issue is that of sexual harassment. It is imperative that our children understand that primitive, animalistic behavior is not acceptable by either gender. It is also important that children understand the role of intimacy in a relationship. Sex and intimacy are examples of topics that can be drastically influenced by an appropriate role model.

The topic of drugs is no different than that of sex. Many parents tend to deny or ignore even telltale signs of substance use or abuse. The operative word with many parents regarding this subject is DENIAL. Sometimes this is out of ignorance, and sometimes it is because the parent also has a problem. If they face the child's problem, they also have to face their own. Well, if you want a scary statistic, suicide and drunk driving kill more teenagers than anything else, and they often go hand in hand. Here, again, educate yourself, and then take the time and effort to educate your child before they do the trial and error method of learning.

All this leads to that all encompassing term–EDUCATION. There is one thing that all parents should agree on. The importance of education can not be emphasized strongly enough. The key to change for the better is our ability to educate our children in all aspects of their lives and then have this skill passed on to the next generation. Down through the ages education has always been valued. Somehow, as a society, we have strayed. Those groups of people who have withstood the test of time by being successful, even in the face of great odds, have done so through education. It is no wonder that when tyrants attempt to destroy a people, they attack the knowledge banks of that people, hoping to destroy the fundamental roots. There is no weapon more powerful than education to eradicate hatred, inequality, and prejudice. We, as a society, need to elevate education and knowledge back to the pedestal that it maintained down through the ages. We live in a society of poor impulse control. Immediate gratification is the generally accepted approach to most situations, and children pick this up at a very early age. Exemplified by what several other governments have labeled a "poor work ethic," whether correctly or incorrectly, the something-for-nothing philosophy permeates our education. Our toys have to be bigger, faster, and more expensive. Our relationships have to be perfect right now. Our children have to attain lofty goals immediately. Children want higher grades. And all of these areas are approached with a sense of entitlement. Our culture seems to resent having to put in time, effort, energy, or money to attain any goals. In the meantime, our education steadfastly slips.

In a genuine effort to provide for our children what we, ourselves, may not have had, or to match what we had, many parents indulge children beyond what is healthy. Adult minds may be appreciative of effort, but the child comes to expect that all things can be accomplished with little or no effort. Eventually, the parent feels used, and a blow-up occurs. But how is a child to appreciate or understand the effort required when this is a learned behavior, and we have provided no opportunity to learn? Guilt and lack of time often play a significant role in the absence of a structure to instill the effort ethic. We feel guilty because we do not have the time that ought to be spent with our children, so we give to salve our own guilt. Education is the key to changing this malfunction, but we need to make the commitment.

Not only do children learn to appreciate everything more readily and to a greater degree when they have had to work for a goal, but the willingness to put forth effort becomes a habit. Few things inspire self esteem like having worked hard to successfully achieve a goal, especially in school. Children take a great deal of pride in presenting the fruits of their labor.

More specifically, we need to do a better job of explaining to our children why all the elements of education are important. Children are often heard to say, "I'll never use algebra, so what do I need it for? No one really cares what happened during the War of 1812, so why learn it? Tell me what job I'll have that I have to recite poetry."

The adult responds, "Trust me. It's for enlightenment. They'll come in handy one day. Besides, it's simply part of your education, and you have to do it. Go finish your homework."

This and similar scenarios have been repeated ever since someone invented passing information from one generation to the next. The problem is that this logic misses the whole point of learning and is not very believable. So why, then, do we have to take all those subjects?

You've decided you're going to get in shape. You go to a person you believe to be knowledgeable and ask for a workout that will get your whole body into proper form—an efficient, mean, lean, fighting machine. This person tells you that she wants you to pick up one 10 lb. weight in your left hand, curl it 30 times, and do this 5 days a week. That's it! "What about the rest of my body?" you ask. You are told that this will get your whole body into shape. Intuition, even with an inexperienced person, tells you more exercises are required to get to the whole body. Exactly the point!

While the brain is not a muscle, it does input, process, and dispatch different types of information in varying ways. Research with ultra-modern technology has recently demonstrated that the brain actually responds positively when it is stimulated, and that assorted types of information stimulate different parts of the brain. "Getting in shape" requires a "variety" of exercises.

Perhaps if the need to take courses in many subjects were presented in a manner that made sense to most everyone, the whole process of education and the motivation to learn would take on a completely new dimension.

In the end, the effort ethic is not a one-shot immunization, but rather a process of education that must begin at an early age. As parents, **WE** are the society and are in control of its future course. That education begins with our parenting skills. There are very few things more important.

How ironic that the experts are now beginning to understand that everything right or wrong with our society really starts in the home, that parenting truly is the most important job there is. So an idea that is considered modern is, in reality, as ancient as humankind.

Chapter VII - Directly From The Source

Ma Cookie

I was delighted when my son asked us to contribute to this practical but sensitive book. I will attempt to make myself "be heard without prejudice."

World! Take notice of this knowledgeable, humorous, helpful publication. I think you will request a sequel to this book after digesting the many recommendations that are suggested regarding parenting. I'm sure I will be accused of being biased. If the truth be known, I'm walking ten feet tall with pride because I am witnessing the fruits of our labor. The years of what we considered "proper parenting" for our children, our son, Drew, and subsequently his wife, Heidi, and our daughter, Gay Denise, and subsequently her husband Hank, have paid off tenfold. We consider ourselves parents to all four adults and are now reaping the benefits of seeing our "dividends"– all our grandchildren – develop into delicious, respectable, caring young people.

The title of this book is quite appropriate for all parents, particularly the part "and other absurd ideas." Why? Because there aren't any set rules on what is "proper parenting." I am a firm believer in the following statement, and I hope it will have some impact on those who read the book. "Anyone can earn their Ph.D. in the field or subject they choose, if they so desire, but you can not earn a Ph.D. in COMMON SENSE."

When we were first blessed with a "young 'un," we attempted to become the perfect parents of our generation. We wanted to give our blessed offspring the stability, love, security, and self esteem that we, ourselves, feel we experienced in our lifetime and was given to us by our own parents. What was taught to us and what was instilled in us as youngsters were traits that we wanted to pass on to our own children as they matured. There was no guarantee, nor will there ever be, that all of what we were

40

doing was beneficial or correct. This point is adequately (thanks a lot) mentioned in Chapter I-Introduction, concerning my outrageous and ridiculous attempt to discipline my "little fellow" for getting out of bed. This brilliant move was on the advice of a friend who was a nurse. Of course, I shall never live that down. However, we all think we are doing the best we can at the time.

I, for one, was exceedingly fortunate to have had the most caring, loving, and concerned parents anyone could have had. As a result, I have made every attempt to convey these feelings to our children and grandchildren from their infancy on. Perhaps, genetically, it comes naturally to me. How my mother and father, Mamma and Pappa, were able to accomplish giving the four of us children the feeling of complete security, emotionally as well as financially (and there were some very difficult times for sure), is no longer a mystery. It is called COMMON SENSE.

When our own children were little, we had to make many moves because of the nature of work that Pa Cookie did. In some respects, it broadened the vistas of education, seeing and visiting different parts of the country. In other respects, the moves created undue stress and tension, particularly for Drew who was in elementary school. He always had to reestablish himself with new youngsters and make adjustments to the new school curriculums and new social settings. At the time, our daughter seemed to fare better since she was younger. Unconditional, demonstrative love and feelings of security were the key words of utmost importance in rearing our children. We tried to make them feel that moving from one state to another was an exciting adventure, and we could all profit from these experiences, educationally, socially, psychologically, and one "slightly" important factor, financially. Of course, there was more bickering than I care to mention between the children while driving long distances, which was quite natural. Parents need to be tolerant. However, both children looked after one another fairly well, and, to this day, remain devoted close friends for which we are grateful. Some periods of time were doubtful, but they came through with flying colors.

The Art of Perfect Parenting

Respect! It seems hard to come by these days, but I feel confident it all HAS NOT gone down the drain. Respect has to be learned and earned. If proper examples are not set by parents at an early age, children become unmanageable. Adults can not expect young folks to understand the concept of respect for one another unless it is practiced within the family on a daily routine basis – no name calling, no belittling, concern for one another's feelings, respect for someone else's opinion. Earn respect from your children by giving them the respect they honestly deserve.

I can not tell you exactly how we developed the trust from our children, but we always tried "to be there" for them when it was necessary. As an example, turning back the clock to 1963 or 1964– "Can we rely upon you to chaperone twenty girls, ages 13-15 with another adult for a week at a resort?" Absolutely! I made it my business to be there for my daughter for this important event because other parents reneged. There was a trust established, and she knew she could rely upon me. In an incident concerning our son, I let a junior high school teacher know in no uncertain terms that I would not tolerate her discrimination toward my son just because he was new to the school and did not abide by her unrealistic and insulting demands. It may have seemed inconsequential, but both children knew I would be there for them if they felt it was important.

Dear Folks, allow your children to develop their own personalities, and don't inhibit them with your own demands and agendas. Praise them, give them emotional support, and teach them tolerance, compassion, and discipline with love! Be their friend, BUT BE A PARENT FIRST. One can become unreasonably authoritative and hinder the development of a sensitive little human being. Guide them, but let them grow as a person.

Enjoy and make the most of parenting for time is a-fleeting, and we should have much to be proud of. We all have our children who can, by becoming beautiful human beings, generally give us fine reasons to stand up and be counted.

Directly From The Source

Pa Cookie

We, Ma and Pa Cookie, are flattered and prideful that our son has applauded our parenting. We thank him for the accolades.

It is said that "opposites attract." Although our views may not always be the same on many subjects, my wife and I have managed to compromise our differences and form a strong union. We placed our priorities in what we believed was a proper perspective, placing our children's development at the head of the list. I am not about to advise or lecture on the obvious, that love and dedication are important factors in rearing children. It would be unnecessarily repetitious to embellish on that subject.

I don't profess to be an expert on parenting. Since I am an optimist, I just did what came naturally and hoped for the best. As for advice to others, I can only state my experiences.

Much of our successful parenting depended upon our cooperation in working as a unit. Good parenting involves total teamwork on the part of the parents. In times past women have been relegated to child bearing, breast feeding, cooking, cleaning, and, time permitting, other miscellaneous chores. They were also expected to meet the needs of the men and to be assistant advisers. Mission Impossible! King Solomon was not called "wise" for nothing. He realized early on that it would take more than one woman to perform all these duties.

Men were considered the breadwinners, main providers, and "heads" of the households. They sired children and were the catalyst for the next generation. Since men were a majority of one in the homes, they became "chief justices of the supreme court." However, the mother was usually the only effective "appellate court" that had the power to reverse any unfair decisions. In today's times the male-female roles are certainly beginning to change toward more equality, and I believe it is for the better.

The Art of Perfect Parenting

In my parenting days, all my non-working time was spent parenting, including sharing and helping Ma Cookie through the many sleepless nights tending to the health needs of our children. However, we were compensated with the joy and pleasure of being parents. The times the children took their first steps or walked, the first school days, the graduations, the confirmations, and the weddings were not always as easy as a walk in the park, but they all were exciting and memorable times. Parents need to cherish those moments.

The degrees of respect between people are endless. One may respect the office of president of a country and hold it in high esteem, but one does not necessarily have to respect the individual holding the office. Demanding respect is inappropriate. Respect is not a right. It is a privilege and must be earned. It is not negotiable. Upon reflection of experiences with our children, we can now understand how we earned that respect. We acted as role models and demonstrated what we meant.

Be devoted parents. When the children were young, they kept requesting a puppy dog. Knowing that I would eventually be the one responsible for cleaning up after the dog and the one to appease the neighbors, I resisted. But that was only for a short time, and I wound up bending to the pleas of "Daddy, we'll take good care of the puppy." Several weeks later I answered a newspaper ad, drove twenty miles to a farm near where we lived in Ohio, and drove back home with a six week old collie pup we named Duke. I shampooed that part of our family for the next fourteen years. Children appreciate devotion.

California was our last and final family move. While on a trip to Yosemite National Park with our children and, of course, Duke, we were driving one dark evening when I spotted a frightened fawn in the middle of the road. I pulled over to the side and picked up the little deer. The children cuddled the frightened animal while a befuddled Duke looked on. We deposited the fawn at the ranger station. A better lesson in compassion for all living creatures could not have even been designed. Teach compassion.

Directly From The Source

Whenever possible, fishing trips were a family affair. Our children loved the outdoors, and we gave them trips galore. Our collection of photos attest to the many wonderful events we enjoyed as a family. Capture all the moments you can, and reflect back on them with your children.

From the time our children were infants we imbued our children with love, compassion, sharing, and caring. We created a favorable image for them to emulate. We, in turn, learned the values of self control and patience which helped us to be "in control" during the children's growing years.

The payoffs are our "dividends," our grandchildren. The "diplomas and degrees" we earned in parenting were rewarded with splendid grandchildren. Drew and Heidi gave us Joshua Barrett and Erit Michele. Our daughter, Gay Denise and her husband, Hank Rams, have blessed us with Elana Gabriella and Ariella Roxanne. Bill, Andy, and Rick by Hank's former union are added bonuses to us.

The love of grandparents for their grandchildren is an unusual, glorious gratification. It is an unexplainable feeling and comfort. Our grandchildren always look forward to Ma Cookie's specialties like delicious potato latke pancakes. Now that Josh and Erit have spread the word, their friends look forward to coming to our home. The love of parenting should extend through the generations. The home of grandparents should be a haven for children and grandchildren of all ages. Let it be an undisciplined retreat for relaxation and an escape from society's hustle and bustle and the daily social pressures, including that from peers. The interaction between grandparents and grandchildren creates a mutual therapeutic, wonderful, comforting feeling.

I stated I didn't want to lecture, However, I can't resist this once. No matter how insignificant the children's daily activities seem, they should be addressed in a positive manner. Take those pictures and videos of birthday parties, Disneyland, baseball and athletic events, family outings, and any other "togetherness" hidden forms of communication. Participation is the key word. You will have the greatest legacy of love and will "glow" over those wonderful and memorable moments when you reach your "golden years." Discount the aches and pains of your aging process and the trials and tribulations of parenting. Successful parenting is life's greatest reward.

Chapter VIII - The Next Generation

Josh

Having been raised in a household with a psychologist and an educational therapist, I've gotten a pretty good idea of what is involved in being a good parent. Not only did my parents use their information with patients, but my sister and I were the unofficial guinea pigs for ideas that my parents had.

I believe one of the first skills necessary in parenting is to be understanding. Children can be very frustrating, and I know there are times where parents might feel like giving up. Remaining "cool under fire" is a skill that is not only necessary in parenting but life in general. Once a person has taken on the responsibility of parenthood, they must follow through. They cannot just simply give up and walk away.

Being a parent is a 24 hour a day job. The information the child gets from the parent and the whole learning process are not limited to nine to five. There is not time off for good behavior. Even when there are times it appears the child is not listening, information is being input that will stay with the child forever.

As far as I am concerned, loving a child without placing restrictions or conditions on the child is the most important action a parent can take. Having been raised in a house in which I knew I was loved just for me gave me a tremendous sense of stability. I always knew I had a safe place.

My sister and I always felt supported in everything we did. This is definitely something that I want to pass on to my children. I believe that my ability to approach all tasks with confidence comes from this support. A child has no fear of making mistakes and is much more likely to attempt new challenges if they feel supported. This also means accepting a person for who they are. Because my parents have taught this to me, I feel comfortable in any situation and with many different types of people.

The Art of Perfect Parenting

My parents are also very open and physical in their love, not only toward us but toward each other. I know that a lot is cultural, but I think that open and appropriate expression of affection is important in the bonding between parent and child. This is one area where being a good role model is a very good teaching tool.

My parents and I are best friends. There may be no way to exactly explain the specifics of this statement, but it is extremely important in parenting. The trust, communication, and love that exists in my relationship with my parents has carried over into all relationships. If parents could give this gift to children, the whole world would be a better place.

The Next Generation

Erit

As a child grows up, they acquire parenting skills. Of course, a child is not aware of everything they are learning. Their parents are just examples of how to bring up children. To a young child everything a parent does is correct. This is why parents need to be aware of everything they are doing that could impact children. A teacher has many responsibilities, as do parents. The teacher is a professional and has been formally trained to teach students. Parents have gone through their entire lives having unofficial training teaching their children. It is also a teacher's responsibility to share the knowledge of the subject matter with the students. The parent has to make sure not to withhold proper parenting skills from their children in the same manner. Hopefully, this will prevent many mistakes, but there will still be mistakes made.

Now, as a reader of this book, one might ask how a fifteen year old knows so much about parenting. I can easily answer the question. My parents have taught me what they know about parenting. They have shared ideas with me about appropriate skills that I will need later in my life. This is not to say they haven't made some mistakes along the way.

My mom and dad have told me to be aware of what others do. They have suggested that I observe as many parents as I can, picking the things I like and dislike. I have chosen to be very aware of everything that MY parents do. Without them knowing, I have figured out many of the skills that they use in daily parenting. These observations have not only added to my own skills, but have also helped me figure out ways to get around problem situations that might lead to trouble.

Good parenting skills really are not just parenting skills alone but are people skills. They will be useful in social and business situations. Developing them into good habits can be very helpful.

One of the most important of the skills is communication. There is no way I can stress how essential communication is to the success of the parent-child relationship. Good positive communication needs to happen on a daily basis. The parent needs to know what makes the child happy and if the child has any problems. All of this needs to be thoroughly discussed.

Good communication also helps build the trust that all children should have in their parents. The child should know that they can ask as many questions as they want, and parents will either have answers or know where to get the answers.

The parent also has to ask questions. However, there is a warning in this question situation. Too many parent questions can seem like the parent is being nosy, can disturb the child, and develop into hostility. A parent needs to know when to stop asking questions. If communication is used correctly, it will be a great advantage in helping the parent provide assistance to the child.

I also favor allowing the child to develop good decision making. This can start at an early age. I remember being given choices and then being allowed to choose one. Even at a young age it will make the child feel a bit more independent. The older the child gets, the more decisions they will have to make anyway. Parents should help children make their own choices. As the child gets older, they will acquire strong decision making abilities. Many times I make my own decisions. My parents always remind me that they trust my decision making abilities. My parents still make the final decisions when it comes to anything that may be harmful or life threatening. It is definitely okay to step in and let the child know that what they are doing is not correct and to offer other choices. The child might get very upset with the choice the parent has made, but they will get over it. The parent should not feel guilty for making the correct decision.

Trust between parent and child in a relationship is crucial. It is an aspect of every relationship. A child needs to know that the parent will always be there. The child needs to know that she can call the parent and that the parents will stop everything to talk to their child. If a child is sick, they need to know that one of their parents will always take care of them. Another example of this trust would be picking a child up from school. If a parent forgets the child or is late, not only does the child feel forgotten, but the trust has been broken. Trust needs to be reinforced throughout the child's life. Sometimes trust can be restored even if it has been substantially damaged by a lot of hard work. Obviously, it would be easier not to break the trust in the first place.

I also know that I do not respect anyone that I can not trust. As a young person I have encountered many untrustworthy adults that to this day I still do not respect. Since they have not proven to me that they are trustworthy, I can not have any respect for them. Many people are aware that respect in general today is a major issue. If respect is lost between a parent and a child, then, most likely, the child will easily disrespect many adults which will present some major problems for the child.

Respect also needs to be given to the child. A parent needs to especially respect a child's privacy, space, and thoughts. If a child wants to be by themselves, then, sometimes, they need to have their privacy respected provided that they are safe. Feelings also need to be acknowledged. The respect for feelings will make the child want to communicate more with the parents.

I think love is the most important part of the parent-child relationship. It brings the parent and child closer together and sets the stage for all other parts of the relationship. There are two types of love. Verbal love is when one person tells the other person that they love them. The other type of love is when words are backed up by actions. If a child is told they are loved and then hugged, they feel secure and protected. Please, don't get me wrong. I think verbal love is very important, but it needs to be backed up with actions. When a child is having a bad day at school or otherwise, they know that someone at home loves them without hesitation or without the child having to do something to get that love. Many times, just knowing this will make the child feel much better. I know there have been many bad days when I thought that people didn't want to be with me.

The Art of Perfect Parenting

When I've come home, I know my parents want to be with me and talk to me. If I have been crying, they have hugged me and reassured me that everything will be okay. This kind of love is one of the strongest feelings. It makes a person happy and feel like they are on top of the world. This understanding of love is important for the child beginning at a very early age.

Support by parents is very reassuring. In this way the child develops confidence. Without support the child might feel self conscious and might even quit at something. I always know that my parents will support me and allow me to make decisions. I believe it helped me grow stronger as a person. The parent still needs to be the final word in what is correct and incorrect.

Communication, allowing for decision making, trust, respect, love and support will aid the child in growing up and in life. It is very important that these skills be passed on from generation to generation. What better person to teach this gift to than your own child? Remember that this is a twenty year long course, so you had better get started right away.

Part
II

The Yellen Behavioral Management Program

If our future lays in the hands of our children, then the vehicle to the future is our parenting skills.

We applaud your decision to actively participate in improving your own skills. Your life and the lives of your children will be greatly improved.

By any measure of success in life, structure is the key to achieving a goal. From beginning to end, efficient and effective structure frees an individual to remain motivated and creative. The business world has recognized this forever. Whenever top executives are asked for the number one reason they are successful, the answer is invariably **structure.**

The **Yellen Behavioral Management Program** is based upon **structure**. The bottom line is it works, but just as important is that parent and child, alike, are happy and content. The unsuccessful attempts and frustrations of parenting will dissolve into a better, healthier parent-child relationship. The Yellen Behavioral Management Program is a unique combination of psychological, educational, coaching, and business concepts. It is a practical, concrete, "hands on" approach to parenting that has been touted by many as being the best answer to imparting values and priorities to children while increasing self-cstccm, self-respect, and accountability for behavior.

You have chosen to invest your love, time, energy, and efforts into your children— our children, and both our and their futures will benefit.

CONGRATULATIONS!

Many of the areas discussed in Part I will be defined more

54

clearly in Part II so that you may have the specifics of "how to." For the most part, well structured behavioral management is effective starting at about age four. Younger children can benefit from a modified and simplified program. Even experts dealing with children who have severe behavioral disorders agree that the most effective means to change is a highly structured program in which children learn to be accountable for their actions. It is not fair to expect this skill of our children when we, as parents, have not adequately taught our children what they need to do.

So sit back, relax, and read. Things in your family are about to change dramatically and permanently for the better.

Chapter IX - The Preliminaries

Critical Issues

Remember that your image as a parent is extremely important. Most of us are very sensitive to how others perceive us. As discussed previously, one of the most devastating put-downs that we can endure is a criticism of our parenting skills. And to the lay person, your child is the representative of your skills. Too many parents like to use the excuse of societal influences or work or a variety of other rationales to absolve themselves of the problems they have with their children. **If they are your children, you are ultimately responsible for them– no ifs, ands, or buts about it!** Attempting to pawn off the responsibility or accountability for your child's behavior on someone else does not cut it. Not to sound gender inappropriate, but moms are generally much more sensitive to the criticisms of others. One may argue the many reasons as to why, correct or not, but it still remains a fact and probably won't change much. I'm reminded of a neighbor we had when our children were little. Her son, who was in elementary school and already prone to delinquency, set fire to the fields next to our house bringing three engines screaming up the street. The mom's only comment was, "If the schools had done a better job of teaching fire prevention, this would have never happened." Obviously, she didn't have a clue.

The consistency of parents is probably the most important element of success. It is essential that any attempt to control your child's behavior not be undertaken until you are absolutely sure that you can be consistent. If there are two parents in the family, there must be agreement or compromise on the terms of the behavioral contract that will be presented. If only one person's parenting needs are being met, the person whose needs are not being met will tend not to be consistent. When children sense disagreement, they use it as a very effective weapon to get their way. In many cases I have to spend considerable time with the parents getting them ready to be consistent. The program is virtually completely effective, **IF** parents are consistent.

A quick lesson in consistent versus random reinforcement is in order. Whenever you want the bear to walk across the room, you reward it with a food pellet for taking the proper step. At the beginning of teaching you reward even if it isn't exactly perfect. This is called "successive approximations." Once the behavior is established, you switch to random reinforcements. As an example, after one step in the proper direction has been instilled by rewarding with a food pellet, the pellet is given randomly every 2-5 times the step is taken. The bear, thinking you haven't seen him, takes the step in a more pronounced fashion, thereby ingraining the behavior even further. Let's look first at how this adversely affects your parenting skills. Let's say you have told your child that she/he can not go out to play because there are only 10 minutes before dinner. The badgering starts something like, "Please, please. I just want to play for a little bit." After about 2-5 times, you pick what you believe to be the easier path to maintain your sanity, you give in. What you have just done is to randomly reinforce your child's behavior. The message that you have so effectively delivered is that it is not a question of whether or not you will give in, it is a question of WHEN and how uncomfortable your child needs to make you before you do give in. Rest assured, you'll be badgered again and probably to a greater degree to start. After all, why use a low flame to boil your pot, when a medium to high flame gets the results so much faster. On the positive side of random reinforcements, do not hesitate to give out rewards in this fashion. "Wow! You did an exceptional job of . . ." followed by the reward. Just make sure it's random. Don't fall into the trap of making it a patterned reward because of pressure. It will lose its effectiveness.

Parents must present themselves to the children as a unified front. Children are master splitters. They will forever use one parent against the other to get what they want and do so on a regular basis. Sometimes this even occurs nonverbally. As an example, I always allow families coming into my office for the first time to take whatever seats they wish. I have a couch that is bordered on both sides by large chairs. In many cases the children have jumped to the couch forcing the parents to sit opposite each other, or one child will sit with one parent on the couch. This clearly identifies the alignment in the family. It also clearly identifies one of the major problems in the parenting that has taken place. Disagreements about parenting should not happen in front of the children. They should be ironed out behind closed doors with no interference and then presented together, with "we" being the operative term. This sends a message that mom and dad are in complete accord and no matter which is asked, the answer will be the same. Doing this will lead to a cessation of splitting.

Kids are great at creating smokescreens to cover the real issues, namely their behavior. This is not to indicate that many of the things brought up by children are not real, only to acknowledge that children are masters at taking the spotlight off themselves by diverting it elsewhere. Parents are often amazed at how sophisticated even 4 and 5 year olds can be. One 5 year old, when confronted with inappropriate behavior, proudly announced, "Daddy, did you know Mommy backed into the corner of the garage today?" The parents immediately turned to each other and began discussing the issue and damage. After putting a stop to the discussion, and pointing out what their child had just accomplished, the parents were astounded. They expressed some doubt until I confronted the child with his behavior, and he smiled and nodded.

Three words are very important in parenting – **Nevertheless, however,** and **regardless**. Your child screams, "I don't like that!" Your reply should be, "Thank you for sharing that with me; HOWEVER, you will still need to do it." I am constantly amazed at how many parents truly believe that there is nothing they can do about their child's behavior. This loss of empowerment either turns to depression or frustration, leading to inappropriate anger response on the part of the parent. You have the power and never lost it. You just have to realize it and use the power wisely.

You've just been told you are unfair. Now you find yourself engaged in a debate over fairness. You have at least 15 years manipulation experience over this young person, but he/she is winning the argument. How many times have you found yourself in the identical position? The situations may vary slightly, but the results are always the same. Your child is calm and collected in a matter of minutes, while you walk away fuming for hours. You have just made the number one mistake in behavioral management-—attempting to justify your position. As a parent, how much time do you spend going to your own room in utter frustration, having just been put in your place by a 5 year old with a trial law degree? Have you been relegated to stares in the mirror questioning your own intellect and aptitude? You are not alone in your disbelief. This scenario is neither acceptable nor healthy for your child. The roots of the problem need to be understood.

Probably the biggest mistake made by parents is engaging in "adult logic" conversations with children. As a rule, children will test limits to define their perimeters, whereas adults, in most cases, have defined these limits. Thus the parent approaches a discussion with an idea of problem solving, but the child has a totally different agenda.

Three criteria usually determine the effectiveness of the "5 year old attorney." It is not necessary that all three be present. However, when they are, the situation is much more difficult to manage.

Take pride that your child's abilities to maneuver around you may be due to her or his intellect. The brighter the child, the faster the tongue becomes sharpened and honed.

A child with good social awareness and self esteem is also a formidable opponent. He or she will be quite astute at picking up non-verbal cues and communication and then using them as part of the arsenal.

The third variable is the level of disharmony within the family system. Especially armed with the first two weapons, a child can easily split opponents apart, utilizing the divide-and-conquer strategy and seasoning it generously with guilt.

Gently but firmly hold fast to all limits. Consistency with a good behavioral program is the most effective means at your disposal.

Let's examine the similarities between behavioral management with your child and a regular poker game. Negotiations with your child are much like a poker game. For those of you not familiar with the card game, much time and effort is spent in keeping secret what the real cards are and bluffing your opponent into submission. For those familiar with the game, you should appreciate the subtle nuances of strategy involved in trying to out maneuver the other person, as well as the awesome feeling of power once you have successfully achieved your goal.

Poker involves being dealt cards, usually some of which are face up and visible but most of which are face down and hidden. Of course, prior to the dealing of the cards is the ante, the beginning stakes that each player is willing to risk. At each stage of the game players bet higher and higher amounts, either because they are convinced that they can win or they do it in an attempt to bluff. The more skilled the player, the more often she or he will bluff, even when the cost factor increases dramatically. In essence the stakes become increasingly greater. Only when you call your opponent's bluff by matching the bet do you get to find out what was really in his/her hand. This is where the bluff takes place. With tremendous amounts already paid, many are unwilling or too unsure to match the bet. They fold their hand without knowing what is in the person's hand, thus not finding out whether they would have really won. This person has been bluffed into submission.

If life with your child seems like one endless poker game, it is probably because he/she has learned to bluff at a very early age. The one significant difference is that most often children do not look at what they stand to lose, thus they are not easily intimidated. Most adults are much more aware of the cost factor, therefore much more vulnerable to the bluff. Know the stakes in advance, and don't be intimidated. **DEAL 'EM!**

It is important that, especially as a parent, you consistently validate your child's feelings. They are absolutely entitled to feel that whatever you have said is unfair as long as they say it in a respectful fashion. In fact, you should tell them just that. Remember Adultisms? Such statements as "You shouldn't be afraid," "You don't really dislike that person," "Don't be angry," or "You don't know what (whatever) is really like" do a tremendous disservice to your child's psychological development and self-esteem. They grow up not in touch with their feelings and have trouble expressing feelings in an appropriate fashion. Certainly the child is allowed to have her/his feelings; however, that does not mean that parents must agree or implement the child's wishes. Neither does it mean that the parent needs to defend his/her position. Your twelve year old blurts out, "I hate your behavior contract." You calmly respond with, "Thank you for sharing your feelings with me; HOWEVER, you will still need to . . ."

Do not engage in a debate. Acknowledge feelings, use one of the three key words, and do not engage in further conversation regarding your recent request. Acknowledgment of feelings does not constitute agreement or action. It is important to remember that you are the parent. A few well-placed "neverthelesses, regardlesses, and howevers", and you are well on your way to taking proper control.

Unconditional love has already been talked about. It is the cornerstone of self-esteem. In no way should any child feel that the parent's love is tied to behavior. Children must feel that they are loved simply for who they are and that there are no strings attached. Again, children must be allowed to express their feelings in respectful terms and to have those feelings validated.

Whether children would like to admit it or not, it is neither good for them to be in control, nor do they feel stable. When the power pyramid is upside down in the family with the children being in control, there is little stability. The children know this and are very uncomfortable. On those occasions that I've had to admit children to adolescent psychiatric units of hospitals, parents are confused and hurt that the children state they like it. Certainly, on one hand they don't like being put in a hospital, but amazingly children are usually aware that they are out of control, so they feel very safe when they have gotten to a place that can contain not only their bodies but their emotions. On the other hand, when parents are firmly in control, with love and fairness, the children may argue briefly, but they feel much safer.

Behavior vs. Cognition

One thing that needs to be made clear at this point is that the actual contract that is to follow only addresses behavior. It is not intended to substitute for good parent-child dialogue or as a replacement for cognitive work that needs to be done with children. Initially, most children behave with little thought behind their actions. This, of course, causes much difficulty for the parent and child, alike. One of the major objectives of this program is to get the child's behavior to coincide with her/his cognitive processing, thinking, so that impulsivity is drastically reduced. To stress the point again, behavioral management is only one component of good parenting.

Let's also separate two words– explanation and excuse. Imagine, "Your Honor, I know that I shouldn't have parked in front of that fire hydrant, but I have 1) a learning disability, 2) Attention-Deficit, 3) many emotional problems, 4) something no one else understands." Take your pick.

"Well, certainly I'd be happy to excuse your parking ticket. How rude of the officer not to recognize your difficulties at that time."

Let's get real, folks. Not even in a storybook fantasy would that scenario take place. As parents, we need to understand the differences between explanations and excuses.

An excuse diminishes accountability for actions. When we excuse behaviors or make excuses for inappropriate behaviors, the message conveyed to children is that they need not be concerned, and there will be no logical consequence for the action. What develops is a child who operates with a feeling of entitlement, who functions in a self-centered fashion without considering the impact of his/her behavior on others.

On the other hand, an explanation examines the series of events or circumstances that led to a particular behavior. It offers a good means of establishing a problem-solving strategy so that similar difficulties can be averted in the future. An explanation in no way removes accountability for someone's actions. Regardless of why a child, or any person for that matter, demonstrates an inappropriate behavior, society is not prepared to simply excuse it.

A more likely response from that judge would be, "Hey, buddy, all of us have problems! Your parking ticket stands! Who's next!"

As parents, we do our children a tremendous disservice by excusing behavior that is less than acceptable. When our children are released into the real world with the philosophy that behaviors can always be excused, they wind up in serious trouble. **ALL** of us need to be accountable for our behavior with no excuses.

There are a number of factors to be considered when examining how to change your child's behavior. While separate, they are interwoven in successful behavioral management.

Yellen's Rule: Action = Reward/Effort. For each individual the definition of rewards and effort may vary. It can be concrete or abstract, money or spiritual, materialistic or idealistic. In any event the bigger the ratio, the greater the likelihood of action, while the lower the ratio the less the chance of action. As an oversimplified example, if I asked you to jump up, run three miles, and return, and there would be a dime waiting on your chair, you'd look at me like I was nuts. There would be virtually no chance of action. Low reward, high effort. On the other hand, if I told you to go to your front door, open and close it, and there would be a $100 bill on your chair when you returned, you would be up in an instant. High reward, low effort, hence excellent chance of action. Remember that you need to figure out what the rewards and efforts are from your child's perspective, not yours. Sometimes just provoking your anger is a very high reward for your child.

Levels of comfort and discomfort are very similar to rewards and effort. The idea behind comfort and discomfort is to structure situations and then allow your child to make the decisions. If I were to present you with two choices, they might be something like the following. In choice number one I put you in a room that has a very comfortable recliner, is about 75 degrees, has your favorite video, and I serve your favorite food. In choice number two I put you in a room that has a hard wooden bench, is about 95 degrees, has the sound of pots and pans clanging, and has only warm water in a glass. I then ask you in which room you would like to remain. Obviously, the level of comfort and discomfort is going to play a major role in your decision as it will in all your child's decisions. Allowing for this decision making removes parents as the target for anger and resistance. The responsibility and accountability for the decision rests on your child, and you get to be a cheerleader instead of a disciplinarian.

Changing the behavioral structure in all environments is the most effective and efficient means to achieve your goals. Changes will occur far more rapidly when there is no avenue of escape. There are certainly those who would differ, stating, for instance, that what goes on in school should have no bearing at home and vice versa. I disagree. When a child feels that all the authority figures are "speaking the same language," results come faster, provided that this is all done with fairness and ego boosting.

Presenting a good role model seasoned with fairness and compassion also allows your child to observe first hand what it is that you are trying to impart. "Do as I say and not as I do" simply cannot work. Parents who take the approach that the parent can do whatever they wish without accountability have set their children up to fail because of the double message. The words do not match the actions which leave children guessing and testing the limits.

The Preliminaries

Perhaps the most difficult task facing parents in implementing a behavioral program is keeping your mouths closed. It seems that most parents have this rather large need to debate an issue with their children until the parents can prove their point. Two factors are on the children's side. Firstly, keep in mind that children have a different agenda. Yours is to be logical and fair, while theirs is to get what they want regardless of the cost. So immediately you are at a disadvantage. Secondly, they are obviously aware, consciously or otherwise, of your need to debate. Hence, the children will keep you engaged in conversation forever if you let them. Seal your lips. After giving your explanation or directive once, simply (hah, hah) stare at them (eye contact is important), do not move any part of your body even to nod, keep your lips together, and be prepared to play the waiting game. Remember that if you give in, you have randomly reinforced their behavior.

Many parents become overly concerned that the program is nothing more than structured bribery. I have a simple answer. Bribery, by definition, means to give inducement to do something illegal or wrong. I would certainly hope that your target behaviors are not illegal or wrong. Therefore, what we are really doing is presenting structured incentives. Action=Reward/ Effort.

Overriding Philosophies

It is of utmost importance that the focus be kept on accountability for behavior. Prior to the beginning of good behavioral management there usually exists a situation in which parents are upset after an incident, but kids are fine. Your little darling has had some inappropriate behavior that you have patiently addressed numerous times. Feeling powerless, you send her/him to their bedroom. While you are seething for hours and frustration continues to mount, your child is happily engaged in some wonderful activity in a room that is not exactly a torture chamber. When two parents are involved, they are usually spending a considerable amount of time pointing fingers at each other in a ritual called "the blame game." Still all the while, the real culprit has escaped accountability. When good behavioral management is implemented, the parents can sit back and let the program take over as the disciplinarian. The child becomes accountable, and if anyone is going to be upset, it should be the child with his or her own behavior.

An important message to instill is that the child makes choices for which she or he is responsible. An appropriate comment when your child blames you for not being able to have some privilege would be, "I'm sorry you CHOSE to have no privileges." This places accountability squarely where it belongs, on the child's shoulders. It also aids in eliminating you as the target for anger.

In order to gently guide your child, you need to make the path of least resistance appropriate behavior and make inappropriate behavior very expensive very quickly. This fits the model of a structured choice and goes the additional step of having an inappropriate choice heavily "taxed." As we examine the behavioral contract, this position will become much more clear.

The message of the whole Yellen Behavioral Management Program is one of emphasis on positive behaviors. Most parents think of a behavioral program as dealing only with those behaviors that are a problem. That means the vast majority of time and energy is spent on negative communication. Good behavioral management places the emphasis on positive behaviors, rewarding them heavily, so that not only does behavior change, but the child feels very good about the whole process. Let's look at the following example of the wrong message being given. On a daily basis little Johnny hears something like the following. "Johnny, how many times have I told you . . . Your teacher keeps telling you . . . Why can't you just . . . I'm really getting tired of . . ."

Little sister Sally comes along with, "Mommy, I got an 'A' on my spelling test." To which the reply is, "Great, Sweetheart." Turning immediately back to Johnny, the comments continue with, "Now Johnny, how come you . . . You'd better learn to . . ."

Hmmmm! What's wrong with this picture? Without realizing it, the message that has just been delivered is that if a child wants attention in that family the easiest way to get it is to act like Johnny. So the following takes place.

> "Johnny, how many times have I told you . . . Your teacher keeps telling you . . ."

Here comes Sally again but this time with a slightly different approach.

> "Mommy."

> "Yes, Sweetheart?"

> "I just failed my spelling test."

Turning and facing Sally, Mom replies, "Sally, how could you do that after all the good work you've done? What happened to you? When did you begin to have trouble? Why didn't you tell me?" Sally has just been reinforced for her behavior (Action=Reward/Effort), and the message in that family is clearly that negative actions bring the most attention. While it may not make sense from the adult logic point of view, it makes lots of sense to Sally. She's learned to play based on the hidden set of rules, and she's been well rewarded for her efforts.

This is also true of good and inappropriate behaviors within the same child. Constructed properly, the program will allow appropriate behaviors to actually aid in eliminating those behaviors that are of much concern by acting as a positive magnet. Much more time and energy needs to be spent addressing the positive behaviors. The goals are that all of the child's behaviors fall in line with the parent's ideas of what is proper, and the family dynamics be structured in such a fashion that there are no mixed messages. Confusion over what is really an underlying value within the family will significantly delay behavioral change.

The Art of Perfect Parenting

Structured Environment

If one were to visualize what was to be constructed to address behavior, it would be a room with rock solid boundaries that would confine the child to the extent that behavior could be controlled while still allowing room for movement in an acceptable fashion. Some parents ask why these boundaries cannot gradually be closed several times until the proper control is achieved. Once you try to control behavior, remember that whether you attempt to close the walls a little bit or a lot, you'll get the same high level battle from your child. Each attempt will be viewed from the child's perspective as a failure. However, if you bring in the boundaries all at once, you will only have one major battle on your hands. Furthermore, each time you open up the walls, it will be viewed by your child as a success.

Not that children should be equated to animals, but this process is similar to horseback riding. If the horse is going down the path, you hold the reins loosely. If the horse starts to go off the path, you pull the reins firmly, holding them tightly until the horse is back on track. As the horse obeys, you gradually let up on the reins. Once on track, however, you don't completely let go of the reins in case you should need to redirect the horse again. This concept should also apply to managing your child's behavior. The program should be gradually expanded but never completely abandoned.

It is important to keep in mind that your child should be free for decision making within boundaries. This is one of several areas with which many parents have difficulty. Once you have structured the choices complete with rewards and consequences, you must allow your child to make the decisions independently. As an example, if your child has earned money and part of the agreement is that she/he can spend the money, your child may choose to impulsively spend $5 on little plastic toys. You should not step in and say, "No." You may have a discussion about values, but by negating the child's decision, you remove the child's decision making skills work so vitally important later on. This structured choice concept has already been discussed in Part I as the 3 year old with sandwich choices. If you are having difficulty with the choices that your child is making, restructure the contract. Do not undermine the child's decision making process.

A good program should be a mirror of real life. The idea is that learned skills can easily and effectively be transferred into real life situations and produce good results. Teaching a child a skill that cannot be implemented in a practical fashion into her/his everyday life is a waste of time. In fact, the whole concept of the behavioral management program is similar to a job description. It defines what it takes to be successful and what consequences will be used if desired goals are not achieved. It gives all parties a clear and objective means of evaluating behavior.

If you are contemplating an allowance, don't, and if you are currently using one, you'll need to discontinue it. The word "allowance" has the connotation of something for nothing. Not long ago I had an eleven year old patient tell me that he could get his parents in trouble because they were violating his rights. I questioned him, and he replied, "They have to clothe and feed me, give me a safe place to live, and give me an allowance." I informed him that he had two of the three correct, but his parents were not obligated to give him an allowance. He assured me that this was common knowledge, but to his chagrin I convinced him that his sources were not correct. The argument usually used in support of an allowance is that it gives children an opportunity to learn how to manage money. Upon closer examination, this view is a fallacy. Let's say that allowance day is Saturday. Your child has been inappropriate (isn't that a nice, tactful way to say 'creep'?) for the majority of the week but wakes up Saturday morning and does everything perfectly with a good attitude. Come time for payment, you are most likely to overlook the rest of the week and pay the full amount. On the other hand, let's say he/she has been wonderful all week but gets up Saturday morning and is just impossible. The tendency is to take it out at allowance time. Furthermore, most parents say that allowance is tied to specific tasks. Here, again for example, the allowance for the week is $5 for which your child is supposed to empty the garbage, feed the dog, do the dishes for two nights, and clean his/her room. They miss one or two of these. What is the consequence–$1, $2, or what? Not having clearly defined rules makes for negotiations every time discipline needs to occur. You don't teach a child or anyone else about money by giving them money that is not tied to specific activities. What you do teach with that type of scenario is entitlement. A very large portion of our young people have been led to believe they are entitled to have things without working hard for them. Children raised without having to be accountable become adults who feel that the world owes them a living. They become angry and frustrated when they can't get what they want, but they don't have the skills necessary to change nor can they accept the responsibility that they must change themselves.

The Yellen Behavioral Management Program is based upon a token economy. That means it uses tokens rather than specific items for rewards and consequences. This is no different a system than money in our society, again a mirror of real life. Money is only a token used to purchase items and privileges. In order to be effective, money must have value. Similarly, there must be a need to have tokens. Imagine for a moment, if you will, that you are told to get a good education, work hard, spend wisely, and save prudently. But you are going to be given a Visa Gold Card that has no limit, and you never have to pay it back. Money becomes meaningless, and you basically spend on impulse. Your care for items begins to deteriorate since you know they can be replaced at any time. It would not take too much time before your work ethic became non-existent. Hey! Still want to give your child something for nothing in the form of an allowance?

It is essential that rewards AND consequences are predetermined. This is accomplished by placing everything into a written contract. Trying to figure out discipline in the midst of an emotional upheaval is a difficult task at best and breeds inconsistency, the downfall of all behavioral management. In addition, by clarifying everything in writing, you will avoid the vast majority of the debate that takes place, because your child knows in advance precisely what is expected. This usually also short circuits much of the testing of limits that children do. When parents ask why children continue a certain behavior, one has only to inquire how many times the parent asks the child to stop. The answer is something like 2-5. Now think for a moment. If you were still a child, and you were unclear on exactly how many times you could get away with something before Mom or Dad REALLY meant business, wouldn't you keep pushing until clarification was made? Voila! You've just answered the question yourself.

This program utilizes rewards and consequences because that, too, is a mirror of the real world. A program that simply rewards positive behaviors or one that only has consequences is not an accurate reflection of what really happens. In the real world, if you make your house payment or rent payment, you get to stay in your dwelling. If you don't make the payment, you don't get to stay. When a child does what he/she is supposed to do, there is a reward, but when they don't, there is a consequence. They can't float in "no person's land" and be expected to change behaviors.

Additional Benefits

While the child's behavior improves, the parents' frustration is significantly reduced. There will no longer be a need to keep trying various methods, including some inappropriate ones that make you feel guilty. A goodly portion of child abuse comes from frustrations in dealing with children's inappropriate behavior. Success is its own best reinforcer and also calms everyone down.

A rise in self-esteem, while listed as an additional benefit, is probably one of the most important agendas related to the program. I hope it has been clearly demonstrated throughout this book that a child's self-esteem is a major factor in success as an adult. From a clinical perspective, low self-esteem is at the root of many problems and can do permanent harm.

Reduction of impulsivity is brought about as the child begins to think about her or his behavior. Again, behavior and cognition are initially at opposite ends of the spectrum at the beginning of the program. The closer these two get, the less the impulsivity.

The Art of Perfect Parenting

You will also find that your own impulsivity with regard to discipline is reduced.

The extension of gratification is a direct result of the reduction in impulsivity. As children become more aware of their behavior and feel confident, they are able to extend the time factor and hold off receiving the reward for an even greater reward. This can be easily illustrated by the "chocolate chip cookie test." There are five regular sized chocolate chip cookies on a table. On another table is one large cookie, clearly the equivalent of about 20 of the others. The children are given a choice. They can have one of the smaller cookies every two minutes for ten minutes, or they can have the larger one in two hours. The rest is obvious. Those children with poor impulse control and the inability to extend gratification will opt for the first choice immediately. Those with good impulse control can put off the immediate gratification in favor of the larger reward. With proper behavioral management and good cognitive work, this skill can be taught.

One of the biggest complaints about children today is that they do nothing on their own. They won't self initiate. Increase in self initiation and motivation is also a primary benefit. This is accomplished by creating the need to begin to do things without prompting. Keeping in mind that Visa Gold card scenario previously discussed, when things are made too easy, self initiation and motivation decline or become non-existent.

Life skills such as savings are a result of extending gratification. As a parent, you are presented with a device that can build self-esteem, reduce impulsivity, help instill confidence, teach life skills, develop a sense of accomplishment and self determination, is fun, and is also inexpensive. What is this marvel of modern times, you ask? The mayonnaise jar!

Actually, it can be a mayonnaise jar, a coffee can, or any other cheap, duplicatable container. The jar has the advantage of allowing the child to see the contents at all times. Let your child pick out what type of container will be used and how it is to be decorated. Each container should be clearly marked with the goal and the amount necessary to achieve it. The objective is to fill the container with enough money or chips to allow them to "purchase" their goal. A few examples of goals might be baseball cards, dolls, theme parks, souvenirs, clothes, etc. A child may have as many jars as he or she chooses, and should be free to transfer funds from one jar to another. With younger children some gentle guidance may be necessary to "prime the pump," so to speak. But trust that they will readily adapt to their newfound form of freedom.

As they are able to fill the jars, the children develop a tremendous sense of accomplishment and, in turn, build self-esteem. Saving helps reduce impulsivity and is a valuable life skill.

But perhaps the real benefit comes from interacting with your child as a facilitator and not a dictator. Isn't that what parenting should be?

I'm often asked how I get children to buy in to the program. I present them with an offer they can't refuse. I give them a hypothetical structured choice with a predetermined level of comfort and discomfort. In the first choice I tell them they will be given a dollar and allowed to watch TV for a half hour. I then ask them what they will have left after the half hour to which they, of course, reply a dollar. In choice number two I tell them they will be given three dollars and TV will cost them one dollar for the half hour. I then ask them what they will have left after the half hour to which they reply two dollars. I then ask them which they like better. Some kids jump at the second choice immediately, while some balk at the idea of having to pay for a privilege that was previously free. After a little thought and coaxing even this group comes around to choice number two (Action= Reward/Effort). Once the whole program is explained and children realize that they can CHOOSE to have many more privileges than they currently have, even though there will be a cost, they are more willing participants. Of course, at this point I don't mention that they could also CHOOSE to lose all their tokens or money and wind up either with no privileges or even in the hole. Part of being a good parent is being a good salesperson.

Blank Template

The actual contract in Chapter 10 is a blank template for your use. It is my firm belief that each parent sets values and priorities for the household. The function of this behavioral management program is not to dictate content, but to aid in the process. As stated in Part I, I personally find it quite offensive that many so called experts attempt to tell all parents exactly how children should be. This program is a highly effective tool to implement your ideas. It is up to you to utilize the tool in the best means possible for your particular circumstances. ANY-THING in the Yellen Behavioral Management Program may be modified to meet your specific needs. The program is not the gospel. Over many years the program has been honed to a sharp edge so that it can be quickly implemented using the examples that are given. But I want to emphasize, again, they are only EXAMPLES. Feel free to use it as it is set up or simply as a guideline.

The second reason that you are presented with a blank template has to do with the active versus passive role of the parent. The majority of programs dealing with children's behavior give you exact steps to follow. You literally have to do no thinking; therefore, you have no vested interest in the program. It is someone else's program that you happen to be following. The likelihood of your continuing the program for any length of time is minimal. Two factors are important in the consideration of designing your own program with some assistance.

Firstly, it forces the parent to clarify in their own minds exactly what they want from the child. So many times parents expect children to have a certain behavior when that behavior has never been addressed, nor is the parent exactly sure of what they want. I sometimes ask if parents expected this knowledge to be transferred by osmosis. By actually writing down and defining appropriate behaviors, there is almost nothing that is overlooked. As an example, if I were to ask you if your child knew what "respect" was, you would probably say yes. But if I were to ask you what you meant by respect, you would probably only give me a few behaviors that fit under that category. That means, in all probability, the chance that you have addressed all the items mentioned later in the book under the definition of respect would not be great, even though you would most likely feel they absolutely should be included. Basically, the process of writing down exactly what you expect brings the ideas to a conscious level, not only for your child but for you, as well.

The second factor is that it is now YOUR program, not only you as a parenting entity, but you as a family. Having spent considerable time and effort defining everything and explaining it to your child, you are motivated to make it work. The resistance encountered from parents usually comes in the form of time and confusion, "We don't have time to do this everyday," or " The program is too confusing." Well, consider this. How much time are you currently spending repeating yourself, yelling and screaming, being exhausted, engaged in conversation about your child either with your spouse or a friend, and dealing with authority figures about your child's behaviors? **AND** is it working? And if it's not working, then you're probably already confused as to why not. You are being presented with a program that should cut the time spent disciplining at least in half and have everybody concerned feel better in the process. What's the resistance? By the way, that does tap into a whole other family dynamic. Many times there is a hidden agenda on someone's part to keep things in disarray, for if the children's behavior were straightened out, much deeper family and personal issues would have to be dealt with.

Chapter X - The Contract

The behavioral contract that follows is your blank template. It is divided into sections for ease of use and each section will be clearly defined with examples to illustrate each step. If you are like me and have little or no patience, you will begin to ask questions immediately. However, if you will go through the explanations and the chapters on anecdotes and pitfalls, I think most of your questions will be answered.

Many people find the idea of a formalized, written contract for children rather difficult. Questions like, "When does a child get to be a child?" are always being asked. The answer surprises many people. Actually, by structuring your child's behavior, he/she is freer to be a child in the truest sense of the phrase. The need for testing limits ceases to exist, and the child feels, as most of us would, much more comfortable with clearly defined goals and objectives. It enhances creativity because time is not spent defining and redefining the process, but is sharply focused on the content of what is out in the real world. To the critics who state that it leaves little room to interact with the world in new ways, two statements can be made. First, it leaves a lot of room for individuality. This was explained in the discussion on erecting solid walls but allowing the child to basically be autonomous, make all the decisions, within those boundaries. Children feel far more stable when everything is clearly defined and they feel the adults are in control. By putting everything in writing you are clearly defining what your expectations are, and the chart can be referred to at any point there is a question. This eliminates the "You never told me that" response to requests. Secondly, our society did the hands off, laissez faire parenting program of the late 60's and 70's. What an utter disaster!!

The actual contract is on the next four pages. It's already laid out in the order it needs to be addressed, so, again, why reinvent the wheel. For purposes of illustration only, the contract will be discussed using chips (as in poker or similar) as the tokens. This is appropriate through about age ten or eleven when money becomes a much stronger motivator. I use chips and money interchangeably depending on the age of the child.

The Contract

Yellen & Associates
psychological & educational services

Behavior Contract

Daily Rewards	Target Behaviors	Consequences Per Occurrence
	Bonus Rewards	
	Bonus Consequences	
Extra Compensation Activities	**Value**	

P.O. Box 3451 • Granada Hills, California 91394 • (818) 360-3078

77

Purchasing List

Short Term (daily)		Medium Term (1-2 wks)		Long Term (Mos.)	
Item	Cost	Item	Cost	Item	Cost

Behavioral Definitions

Target Behavior	Definitions

The Contract

Target Behavior	Definitions

Target Behavior	Definitions

Signatures:

X_____ Date:_____   X_____ Date:_____

X_____ Date:_____   X_____ Date:_____

The Contract

Target Behaviors

Target behaviors are those behaviors that you will be insistent about. These are not optional for your children. Notice under this section on the first page of the contract that there is only one small space to write. You will define each target behavior specifically starting on page two. Suggestions for ideas appear in the next chapter, not surprisingly entitled "Definitions." I have selected the five most commonly used target behaviors–respect, household, hygiene, school, and sibling. Feel free to add whatever you determine to be appropriate target behaviors for your household. Some others that have been used by parents have been religious school, morning behavior, manners, after school care, and car pool or bus behavior. A rule of thumb is that anything that you want to address on a consistent basis should be listed as a target behavior. As discussed, target behaviors should include all behaviors, not simply the ones that are a problem. Remember that the long term goal is to bring all of your child's behaviors into line.

To the left of the target behavior column is the reward column, and to the right is the consequence column. All target behaviors have a reward and a consequence attached to them. But if you will notice, there is one very significant difference. Rewards are a set amount daily for meeting the entire target behavior, while consequences are per occurrence of a problem behavior. In other words, as an example let's say that the daily reward for respect was 10 chips, while the consequence for each occurrence was 5 chips. A child would receive 10 chips for the day for having been appropriate for respect, not each definition of respect but the entire target area of respect. However, if he/she were disrespectful 8 times that day, they would lose 40 (8x5). This follows the idea that "the path of least resistance is appropriate behavior, and inappropriate behavior becomes very expensive very quickly."

The token economy tally should be done daily. The exact method will be explained a little further in this chapter. Extending the tally to the end of the week causes a dilution of the effects of the contract. Once, again, many people complain that it would be difficult to do daily, but my reply is always that they are spending the time in one way or another already, and it has not been effective. Why not spend the time in a productive fashion?

All the amounts on the contract are predetermined. This allows for rewards and consequences to be determined in a calm atmosphere rather than at the height of emotions when neither parent nor child tend to think rationally.

All rewards are accompanied by much celebration and enthusiasm. The celebration and enthusiasm act as rewards themselves. Eye contact, body language, facial expression, and voice intonations all carry a lot of weight when it comes to motivation. Don't ever underestimate the power of a good smile. Consequences, on the other hand, are accompanied by nothing – no emotionality, no lectures, no frowns, no other actions. In that way the contract is doing the disciplining rather than you. You are helping remove yourself as the target.

A good rule of thumb for figuring ratio amounts is that the consequence per occurrence is approximately 50% of the daily reward for any given target behavior, such as 10 chips for a target behavior and 5 chips per consequence for violations. Some parents like to have all the rewards for the different target behaviors the same, i.e. 10 chips for each behavior. Other parents like to place greater importance on one or another of the target behaviors by making them 20 or 30 chips. The first is easier, while the second allows you to emphasize one behavior category over another. The choice is yours, and both seem equally effective.

It is very important to note that second chances act as enabling behavior. When parents say things like, "Now this is the third time I've had to ask," or "I'll give you one more chance," they only serve to prolong the episode and give the child the wrong messages. To be most effective, rewards and consequences are given the first time, every time.

The Contract

Bonus Rewards

The two purposes behind Bonus Rewards are to establish consistency of appropriate behavior and to provide a means of rewarding behaviors that were over and above what is called for in your contract. In this way you are providing an additional motivational factor, another sales point for the program.

A good marker for short range consistency is three days. Especially for children that have moderate to severe behavioral difficulties, three days is long enough to require some thought but short enough to appear achievable. What we really want is to remove the roller coaster ride of appropriate and inappropriate behaviors, and begin to have almost every day be a rewardable one. Remember, if you want a behavior to be consistent, reinforce it.

Don't ask for perfection in the behaviors. That becomes a set up for failure. As an illustration in setting up bonus rewards, a guideline would be no more than 6 consequences cumulative for three days, i.e. 3-3-0, 3-2-1, 5-0-1 etc. Using 5 chips as the consequence, we could translate this in to a maximum of 30 chips or less in consequences for three days. If that goal is achieved, then you could give a bonus reward of 50 chips. Obviously, you are placing a big premium on consistent behavior.

Some parents also like to put an extended bonus reward for holding it together for 7 days or more. The same principle of allowing for a certain number of violations cumulatively would apply, i.e., no more than 15 consequences in a week would earn a bonus of 100 chips. In this manner the idea of consistent behavior is extended even further.

Another area to be used for bonus rewards is that of cooperation, especially when there is more than one child. When children do something together in a cooperative fashion, it takes less time and there is a premium placed on that cooperation. As an example, a little later in this chapter the category of Extra Compensation Activities will be discussed. These are things that children can do to earn extra chips. So, for instance, if the children received 3 chips for a particular extra task, by doing it together they would get 4 chips. This means they can do it in less time and receive a bonus for cooperating.

Bonus rewards, as with all rewards, should be accompanied by much enthusiasm and celebration. They become much more effective. Also give a Bonus Reward for anything "above and beyond."

Bonus Consequences

One of the purposes of having bonus consequences is for having a means of coping with a child who uses up a reasonable allotment of consequences (chips) in a short period of time. Remember that part of your agenda is to make appropriate behavior the path of least resistance and to make inappropriate behavior very expensive very quickly – the ole' comfort/discomfort formula.

Parents usually like one hour, one day, and three days as markers for assessing additional penalties. As an example, having 5 consequences in one hour (losing 25 chips) would bring an additional surcharge of 25 chips. So the child can lose 5-10-15-20, but if they get to losing 25, then they actually lose 50 (25 for consequences and 25 for bonus consequence). The other markers might be having 25 consequences in 3 days, bringing about an additional penalty of 150 chips or having 75 consequences in one week, losing an additional 400 chips. You can adjust it any way you wish, but it is guaranteed to catch the child's attention. Most kids will initially push the consequences just up to the bonus consequence level but won't go beyond because it is too costly.

A second benefit of bonus consequences is what I call No Fault Insurance. Many households suffer from the "Wet Towel Syndrome." Your children use a separate bathroom. Now, you haven't used their bathroom, you've had no guests in the house, and, to your knowledge, the house is not inhabited by ghosts. But, lo and behold, there is a wet towel on the floor of the children's bathroom. You ask one child, who denies responsibility and leaves. You ask a second child, who denies responsibility and leaves. Guess who winds up picking up the wet towel – and mumbling something about being sick of doing this over and over? Rejoice! You are going to implement No Fault Insurance. Since you have no knowledge of which party is responsible, ALL parties are responsible. That's correct. Everyone is assessed a consequence. In this case you would simply announce that all will have a 5 chip penalty assessed. Remember that this is only done when it cannot be determined who is at fault or if no one will take responsibility for the problem. Even though a consequence, there is still a lesson in cooperation to be learned by the children. One child walks past the bathroom and spots the towel. He/she thinks, "That's not mine. I'm not going to pick it up. But wait. If I don't pick it up, I'll lose chips also." Many parents are concerned that one child will then go yell at the perpetrator. No problem. If you hear yelling or screaming, the same No Fault rule applies. It even applies during a cooperative effort. Yes, they get the bonus for doing something together, but if you hear yelling, go in and announce that since you do not know who started the yelling, they both are fined. Certainly, they will still have earned the bonus for cooperation.

The bonus consequences are also to be used for any extraordinary circumstance not covered in contract. Simply include as a catch all phrase something like, "All items requiring a consequence not covered in the contract will be handled in a manner to be determined by the parent and then to be included as an addendum to the contract."

Extra Compensation Activities

At the bottom of the first page of the contract is the category that is responsible for two important functions. Firstly, it provides a means of children making up for consequences by doing extras. Secondly, it addresses self-initiation as had been previously discussed. Even with no consequences children have an opportunity to "figure out" how they can earn extra chips for the things they want.

The Art of Perfect Parenting

Notice that the area under the consequence column is grayed out. There are no consequences for not doing these activities. They are EXTRA. Parents often ask what the difference is between this section and Target Behaviors. Any behavior that you insist upon would fall under Target Behaviors. Anything that you would wish to offer as a means of your child earning extra would fall under Extra Compensation Activities. What is a mandatory behavior in one household, let's say putting dishes in the dishwasher, may be only an optional task in another and vice versa. It all depends on what is proper for your house. Some examples are sweeping the porch, setting the table, folding laundry, shining shoes, washing or assisting with the car, gardening, preparing recyclables, watering plants, vacuuming a particular room, extra book reports, extra credit in school, and anything you would like to see them do on their own. I like parents to list about twelve to fifteen tasks with assigned values. Kids may say, "Yuck! I don't want to do that." Your comment is that it is not something they have to do, and they are certainly free to choose not to. Don't put anything on this list that you are not willing to make optional. Again, if you want the behavior from your child, reward it.

Relative values have to be considered. With 10 chips used as an example of an amount of a daily reward for a Target Behavior you would not want to make vacuuming the living room worth 25 chips, because what you are telling the child is that one task that takes about 15 minutes carries two and one half times the value of and entire day of a Target Behavior. We go back to Action=Reward/Effort and Comfort versus Discomfort. You have just lessened the consequence for inappropriate behavior. Just for relative value comparison, if your contract has 10 chips as the amount for daily reward for a particular Target Behavior, Extra Compensation Activities should be somewhere between 2 and 5 chips depending upon the task. In extraordinary circumstances, when the task takes significantly longer, as in one or two full days, the amounts can be increased.

The Contract

The Token Exchange

In terms of modifying behavior, the manner in which the token exchange takes place is exceedingly important. We know there are three learning channels for all people: visual (seeing); auditory (hearing); and tactile (touch). Some people are strong in all three, while others have a deficit in one or more. By using all three in the token exchange, two things are accomplished. We insure that the information is getting across, and we begin to strengthen any weak channels. To illustrate, using the example amount of chips, you would say, "Here's ten chips for respect" as you physically transfer the chips across the table. You would repeat the process for each of the target behaviors and the extra compensation activities. The child is seeing the chips, hearing the amounts, and is able to touch the chips. In this manner you are connecting behaviors to specific amounts, thereby eliminating the generalizing that so often takes place, as discussed, with an allowance.

Always specify the amounts for positives first. Even if the child will wind up losing all the chips, give out all the positive reinforcers first. In this manner the child has a relatively large stack of chips in front of her/him. Remember that each reward is celebrated enthusiastically including body language and facial expressions.

Next come items from the purchasing list (to be discussed shortly). These are handled in a simple, business-like fashion since they are privileges the child chose to purchase. Finally, in the same manner as the rewards, all consequences are delineated, one at a time, with the transfer of chips taking place after each single occurrence. "This morning you left your dishes at the table. That will be 5 chips." The child is hearing the amount, must visually address the chips, and must touch them in order to transfer them back to you–again, all three learning channels. In addition, there is a big impact on the child by seeing a large stack of chips dwindle rapidly. If the child goes in debt by using up more chips than he/she has available, "into the red," he/she owes the following day. You will still give them all chips from positive behaviors first, but you will then deduct whatever is

owed for being in debt from the previous day(s) prior to purchase items or consequences for that day.

Do not allow your child to make this process a simple money
exchange. "Mom, I earned 60 chips and lost 40, so just give me
the 20." This diminishes the effects of the program, shifting
away from a behavioral focus and making it a simple math
lesson. We know that the most effective means of learning is
to "overlearn." Normally, there will be 8-10 positive exchanges
each day and 8-10, sometimes more, negative exchanges. This
means you are literally repeating the process probably 15-25
times daily, translating to 80-150 times weekly. This is called
covert persuasion. Your real agenda is covered. If you actually
tried to tell your child the same thing that many times daily and
weekly, overt persuasion, there would be a major battle. Covert
persuasion is much more subtle and so much more effective.

If you will be using chips, use different colors for different
children. This serves as an anti-theft and anti-extortion mecha-
nism. The older children cannot coerce the younger ones, or
"borrow." It makes everyone completely responsible and accountable for themselves. By the way, some always ask what
kind of chips. Standard poker chips will do. I've even had
parents go to the trouble of making their own out of tiles, wood,
or plastic. Even that can be a means of involving the children by
having them help make their own tokens.

This type of repetition replaces inappropriate behavior with
parent-defined appropriate behavior. You have selected what
behaviors you feel are appropriate and are now going to consistently reinforce these.

This is also a good place to teach children about savings and the
value of things. You are also providing a method by which
children have the freedom to make choices and begin to problem
solve. This adds to self esteem in a large way.

The Contract

The Purchase List

You will find this section on the second page of the behavioral contract. Try to keep in mind that costs must have relative value. If prices are too high, children give up because they view everything as unachievable. If prices are too low, children learn that nothing has real value. The basic premise with younger children is that if they have no chips they have no privileges. With older children, the same ideas are applied to money. As previously discussed, some children balk at the idea of having to purchase things that were previously free. If your sales job was effective, there won't be as much resistance. If it wasn't, remember "Nevertheless, However, and Regardless." This is where closing in the boundaries completely is really used in the practical sense. EVERYTHING becomes a purchasable item. Then, as behaviors begin to fall in line, you can gradually loosen the reins by having less of the short term privileges purchased.

The purchase list has been divided into three sections—short, medium, and long term purchases. By structuring the contract in this fashion, you are beginning to teach sequencing and the extension of gratification. What you will actually do is control your child's activities by the purchase price. Because YOU determine what is best for your household, you will be regulating the activities without becoming the target. This is the advantage of structured choices. Let's use television as an illustration. In some homes parents feel comfortable with no more than two hours per day, in some homes parents insist upon no TV during the week at all, while sometimes the parents don't have a problem with the child watching more if all chores and homework are done. That choice is yours. If you were to tell your child that she/he can only watch two hours per day, you are regulating the behavior. But if you use a cost factor, the child must self regulate. With the amount of chips we're using to illustrate values, a child can probably accumulate 50-70 chips in a day for appropriate behavior if we include extra compensation activities. If you wish to limit TV to the moderate range, you can have a cost factor of maybe 10 chips per half hour. This would more than likely result in your child only having enough chips to watch about two hours and still be able to buy other privileges. However, they may CHOOSE to spend all chips on TV for that day. Don't worry. It won't be that way every day because it's too expensive. If you want a tighter limit, make the purchase price higher.

On the other hand, there are some activities that you would probably wish to encourage like riding a bike because it is good exercise. You could consider making this about 5 chips per hour, thereby making it much more accessible. Many ask why something as important as exercise should have a cost factor. Most children consider play as something important, so it becomes a good motivator. But the bottom line question is if your child is completely disrespectful, has done nothing around the house, and has ignored schoolwork, should he/she be allowed to leisurely go out and play? For most the answer is, "No way!" Here, again, rather than you being responsible for the behavior by saying they have been inappropriate and are "grounded," the contract becomes the disciplinarian. By placing a nominal amount on an important desired activity, you are making it very accessible, but are also maintaining good control in the event the child's behavior is out of compliance, and you are not becoming the target for anger.

Some examples of short term (daily) privileges to be purchased are: TV; Nintendo or other electronic games; the telephone (emergencies are excluded but be sure to specify what to do in an emergency); stereo; extended bedtime; any activities performed on a daily basis including toys, bike riding, play time, etc. Approximate costs for short term are usually the equivalent of one target behavior daily reward for a given time period (i.e. 10 chips might be the daily reward for a target behavior so you would use 10 chips per 1/2 hour of TV in our given example). If you were going to use money and your daily reward were 50 cents for a target behavior, then you could use 50 cents per half hour. Remember that you can adjust cost factors up or down to meet your needs and priorities.

Examples of medium term (1-2 weeks) purchasable activities are restaurant; video rental; movies; sleepovers (either a friend at your house or your child at a friend's). Medium term approximate costs are 8 to 20 times reward for one target behavior. Here again using 10 chips as the reward for one target behavior, the range would be from 80 to 200 chips for the activity depending upon which would be normally more costly.

Examples of long term (months) purchasable privileges might be: theme park; major purchase such as bike, roller blades, electronic game, etc.; and major trip. Approximate costs might range from 100 to 200 times the reward for one target behavior. In our illustration case that would be somewhere between 1,000 and 2,000 chips. Before your jaw hits the ground about how high a figure that is, let's look at some numbers. Once your child comes into compliance with the program, he/she will be earning and keeping about 60-80 chips per day, which is some 400-550 chips per week, which is 1,500 to 2,500 chips per month. Remember that they are free to use the chips in any fashion you have outlined in the contract. If they choose to save all the chips for theme park privileges, and you make that item only 500 chips, you might be going to Disneyland every week to two weeks until its novelty wears off. Keep in mind that if you say no, you are reverting back to taking responsibility and accountability for behaviors and removing decision-making and problem-solving opportunities. This is why you will structure everything in advance and have the child make the decisions with your full support. The importance of your planning of relative values now becomes very obvious. Once you commit to a program, you must set an example by sticking to it as much as possible. Proper planning helps.

It is also a good idea to set up an exchange ratio of chips for money so that the value of money becomes important. For instance, you might make each chip have a value of one cent for younger children, 5 to 10 cents as they get older. This allows them to directly purchase things in a store. The exchange only goes one way, however. They can trade chips for money but not vice versa. This takes care of the problem that develops when Grandma or Aunt Sally or Uncle Hank give the kids money for occasions. Otherwise, you would have a situation where you have made your child toe the line for a period of time, and then along comes, "Grandma just gave me $25, so I want 2,500 chips." They would then be able to go a very long time without feeling the impact of consequences. With older children who are using money for tokens anyway, the problem is not as bad as it would appear since they have to pay actual value for most things like movies, fast food, etc. You could certainly specify that privileges can only be purchased with earned money. This prevents raiding the regular savings accounts.

I always remind parents of young to middle adolescents that parents have tremendous leverage in the form of driving privileges. Since this is a prime motivator, you can tie certain behaviors directly to it. Many parents take the position, "No B's, no keys." While the concept is accurate in that tying driving privileges to grade point averages (GPA) is acceptable, the child's capabilities need to be considered as some may not be able to maintain a 3.0 GPA because of abilities and disabilities. For many a 2.5 or 2.75 would be more realistic. Keep in mind that if the goal is genuinely viewed as unattainable by the child, there will be no effort extended, thereby defeating the whole purpose. The GPA should be applied to both getting and keeping the driving privileges. If you are financially able, you can also offer bonus incentives for higher GPA's such as gasoline expenses, or help with insurance.

As previously discussed, teaching children to save is an important life skill. This is the ideal portion of the contract with which to accomplish your goal. In the case of adolescents, actual savings accounts, perhaps even checking accounts, serve as excellent learning tools. Remember that the child is free to shift funds from one account to another. This corresponds with the idea that they are free to operate within a defined boundary. Your interference in this process puts you in the position of responsibility for behavior, again. While it may be irritating that "money burns a hole in their pockets," you need to let the process of behavioral management take its course. Modify the contract, but don't interfere in the process.

As behaviors fall in line with what you feel are appropriate, there will be a gradual shift to long term purchases. Short and medium purchases will serve as rewards. "Mary, your behavior has been excellent for six weeks now, so I'm going to remove TV (or others) from the list of things you have to buy. Congratulations!" Now whatever tokens would have been used to purchase TV time can be applied to medium and long term items.

The important point is to never drop the entire program. You can loosen and tighten the reins as necessary, but if you drop the entire program, it will be much more difficult to implement. IF IT AIN'T BROKE, DON'T FIX IT. I can not tell you how many times parents have brought the family back to see me for a "30,000 mile attitude adjustment" only for me to discover they have dropped the entire behavioral management program. When I inquire if it worked well when used, the answer is invariably and enthusiastically, "Yes." When I ask how long the child's behavior has been on the decline, the answer always coincides with the time that the behavioral program ceased, give or take a week or two. As stated throughout, virtually the only time the program is not effective is when the parents are not consistent. The best tool in the world is useless if it just sits in the box. No parent is perfect. We have already established that. But make every attempt to maintain the consistency, and your entire family will reap the benefits.

At this point what is left is homework. You will need to carefully define all of your target behaviors, bonus rewards, bonus consequences, extra compensation activities, and purchase list items. This whole process is only a structured tool for YOUR values and priorities. By giving examples used over years of working with families, I want to make the process easier but leave the ultimate creativity to you, the parent. I've also included a chapter on some of the pitfalls of setting up contracts so that hopefully you will be able to avoid them. Make sure that in your first shot at implementing the program you include the catch-all phrase "to be evaluated in two weeks" at the end of the contract. It is not advisable to change the contract once it has been established because it gives the child the idea that rules are a one way street. As a role model, if you can change at a whim, why can't they? That is why you need to be very careful about what you put in and how you word it. By including the catch-all phrase you can close the loopholes in a short period of time. If you are not an attorney, you may feel like becoming one. If you are an attorney, why are you losing your cases to your child?

Chapter XI - Definitions

I've chosen five of the most commonly used target behaviors to illustrate the program: respect; household; hygiene; school; and sibling. Please pick what definitions you would like to include in your contract. Also remember to include any additional target behaviors that are of importance to you and to clearly define them, as well. You do not need to put in amounts for rewards and consequences in this section since that has already been done on the front page of the contract. You will simply be identifying those behaviors that are desired and those that will cause a consequence. Try to keep the wording age appropriate. For younger children you may even wish to have pictures. On pages two, three, and four you will list the target behavior once on the left hand column and all applicable definitions of that behavior in the right hand column. More pages may be added to allow for more definitions by duplicating page three and inserting it. Again, keep in mind that the more precise you are at this point, the easier your job will be, the less you will have to modify later, and the more you can relax (believe it or not, that word is still included in the parent dictionary).

Respect

Please note that the first three definitions have a "10X" next to them. This indicates that the consequence for these violations is 10 times the norm, or in our illustration of 5 chips per occurrence, 50 chips. This is because most parents feel that violations of this nature are so much more significant than others. If you wish to make them only equal to a normal consequence, just eliminate the "10X" designation, and if you want to be tougher, use 20X or 30X.

Honesty, No lying (commission vs. omission) 10X- It is very important that children understand that neither form of lying is acceptable. Commission or committing a lie means actually telling something that is not true. Omission or omitting means that either they are leaving out a portion of the facts or pulling something out of context. Let's say your child ate three cupcakes before dinner. You ask, "Did you eat a cupcake?" The child's answer is, "No." Well, technically they are right. They did not eat "a" cupcake, they ate three. This is a lie of omission. Both forms of lying need a heavy consequence.

No stealing 10X- Taking something that does not belong to them without permission is not appropriate. Don't accept the excuse that they were just borrowing the item.

No intentionally dangerous physical action 10X- This is a broad statement that includes hitting, kicking, throwing objects, pushing down stairs, playing with matches, playing with knives, endangering the lives of others, going up on a roof, etc.

Do something first time asked- Remember that second chances act as enabling behavior. Parents tell me that they would love to have children do something the second or third time asked. That is not acceptable. Children need to do something the first time they are asked and should be assessed a consequence for anything past the first time.

Do not ask one parent then the other- This stops the splitting and manipulating of parents. Be on guard, especially at the beginning of the contract.

Take "no" for an answer- Exactly what part of NO don't you understand? Once you have said no, that is final. The prolonged debating must stop.

No screaming, yelling, or raising voice - Of course, by parents' standards.

No profanity - Okay, Mom and Dad, this means you, too.

No stamping feet or pounding fists - Basically, this is to eliminate the standard temper tantrum displays.

No socially unacceptable gestures - This includes giving someone the finger, or anything that you consider an impolite gesture.

No interrupting - No explanation is necessary.

No inappropriate body noises -Without being gross, we all have an idea of what this means. Boys are notorious for these types of behaviors.

No slamming doors or other objects - Children must learn to deal with anger in socially and parent-defined acceptable ways. They can have their feelings, but not at someone else's expense.

No mimicking, mocking, or provoking - This generally occurs with siblings, but can be with friends and relatives.

Please and Thank you - Good manners, in general, are important.

No making faces - This is separate from just gestures. It includes everything from a disgusted look to eye rolling.

No sarcasm - Nothing seems to start a fight faster.

Appropriate greeting for people - Children should know that they need to greet others in the proper way.

Must respect personal space and belongings - While this is very general, the concept is very important. By the way, include YOUR personal space and belongings with this.

Household

Many tasks will vary from household to household. As discussed, in one house certain tasks may be required, while in others they are extra. Whatever suits your needs belongs here, but all children should have some responsibility for portions of the household. A question I am often asked is whether children should be made to clean their rooms. Some parents insist since the room is in their house, children will maintain rooms in the same manner the rest of the house is maintained. Other parents feel that the room should be a sanctuary for children and just close the door. A reasonable compromise to this dilemma is to have the room, closet, bathroom, etc., cleaned twice weekly by some chosen day and time. This allows for independence but also prevents total disaster as well as grunge and mildew growing under the piles.

Since things need to be done to your standards, write out a checklist. Your version of a clean bathroom and your child's version are probably not quite the same. A list eliminates an argument before it starts. As an example, you might photocopy a list that says toilet cleaned with cleanser inside and out, seat cleaned top and bottom, sink cleaned with cleanser, mirrors cleaned, bath or shower cleaned with cleanser and rinsed, drawers straightened, toilet paper filled if necessary, and floor mopped. In this way, every time your child goes to clean the bathroom, they can bring back the list checked off. There is no question about what is expected, hence no fight.

Everything in room in proper place, neatly

Everything in closet in proper place, neatly

Everything in bathroom in proper place, neatly

Bed made

Take dishes away (optional rinse and/or load)

Hang up jackets

Meet family obligations

Help when asked

Any needs specific to YOUR household

Definitions

Hygiene

Hair

Teeth

Bath/shower

Washing hands, face

Clean clothes

Nails

School

As previously mentioned, there are many so-called parenting experts who suggest that school and home should be separate, that parents should be responsible for home and let school officials be responsible for education. They even joke that if a teacher can send a note home that the parent must help the child complete an assignment not finished in class, the parent should be able to send the hamster cage to school with a note saying the teacher should help the child since he/she was unable to finish at home. The teacher will only have your child for a brief time. You will be your child's parent for a lifetime.

Heaven forbid that your child would require surgery, but if that were the case, you would be there with no questions asked. You would not send them to the hospital alone and leave everything to the doctors and nurses. If someone were to question why you found it necessary to be present, you would look at them in utter disbelief that such a question would even be posed. Most of us would not even bother explaining anything to that individual because simply asking the question indicates this person could not begin to comprehend the great responsibility of parenthood.

In fact, most of us are closely involved in all aspects of our children's lives to insure that they are receiving the best, the most comprehensive care for as long as may be necessary. Not only are these the responsibilities of parenthood, but they are the privileges as well. To watch your child achieve is one of life's greatest pleasures. You need to enjoy more of those pleasures by structuring the lives of your children for more success, not just a minimal amount.

With the exception of family dynamics, catastrophic events, and a few other issues, nothing impacts a child's life in the long run greater than her or his education. It may not have the momentary life or death impact of that major surgery, but it certainly is a matter of life. Studies have shown that family and education are two of the most significant factors in success.

Why, then, do many parents choose not to be involved in their child's education? Why is the process simply left to the educators? This is certainly not to diminish the fine professionalism that exists in most educational institutions, but just as the doctors and nurses are professionals and you are still there for support in every way possible, it is just as important to be there for your child's education in every way possible during the entire course of her/his educational career. If you haven't already, become and stay involved. If you have, **BRAVO!**

Home needs to be a safe haven for children. You can emphasize education and still be very supportive and understanding. There are times when your child legitimately will have complaints about school. The child should be listened to and, when appropriate, supported in their position at school. Most teachers are professional, dedicated, and really care, but sometimes we have found those who are not. The children need not to feel helpless in their education. Sometimes the pressure just comes as part of the process. It is not the teachers, the students, or the parents.

As an example, the school board realizes that it has only weeks to implement plans that were laid out last September, so they place pressure on the district administration to get everything in before year's end. The district administration, in turn, places pressure on school administration, who places pressure on teachers, who, of course, put pressure on students. But, it doesn't stop there, because your student, frantically hitting the panic button, uses the most convenient and comfortable target available–YOU.

You cannot stop the trickle-down pressures of school year's end, but you can take steps to lessen the impact and negative effects. Your child may begin to feel overwhelmed as the pace picks up. Two actions are very important. Firstly, validate your child's feelings. Let him or her know that you understand the turmoil. Secondly, sit down with your child and work out every possible thing he or she can think of that is upcoming. Next, come up with a plan and time-line to address each issue. This will certainly be done at an age appropriate level, but your child will be given the feeling that he or she is not in it alone.

Particularly with students who have finals as part of their schedule, pressure begins to mount. This is not to say that the process is not beneficial. Learning to cope with increasing pressure in an efficient manner without producing a lot of detrimental effects is an important skill. But at times it can become so stressful that it becomes a negative. When possible, give support and present strategies to help your child cope so that the situation becomes a positive rather than a negative.

This educational scenario can then be applied to other aspects of life. Education is important not only for its intrinsic value but also as a means of preparing for other life tasks. Help your child learn to take the trickle-down pressure in stride.

Charts - I have included one of the charts we use in the office. It is very simple, but provides daily communication from school to home. It is the child's responsibility to carry it both ways. With older elementary school children we replace the happy and sad faces with "on target" and "off target." Teachers like the simplicity because it takes literally ten seconds to complete, but comments may be added. With the elementary school children I usually advise that if the chart comes home with all happy faces, they get the 10 chips for the entire target behavior. Each sad face is a 5 chip consequence. This streamlines the process.

The Art of Perfect Parenting

WEEK:

PLEASE CHECK COLUMN FOR 1 WEEK ONLY	ATTITUDE		WORK COMPLETED		QUALITY OF WORK		SELF CONTROL		PEER INTEGRATION	
MONDAY										
TUESDAY										
WEDNESDAY										
THURSDAY										
FRIDAY										

ADDITIONAL COMMENTS:

YELLEN & ASSOCIATES

PSYCHOLOGICAL & EDUCATIONAL SERVICES • (818) 360-3078

Definitions

Progress reports/report cards - With middle school and high school, you can use a weekly progress report and set up rewards and consequences in a similar manner to the above charts.

Assignment sheets - We recommend this for all students. Notice, this does not say "homework sheet," it says "assignment sheet." Every assignment is written down with the date assigned and if applicable, the due date, date returned, and grade. This includes watching movies or reading assignments. In essence, you will know what goes on in class.

Many parents are so focused on the end product that they lose sight of the beginning. Study skills are sequential. What occurs at the beginning of the study process affects the outcome.

Quite often the only discussion regarding schoolwork revolves around the progress report or report card. The end result of the study process is obviously the most significant, but the foundation of the study process determines the quality and structure to follow. The beginning of that process is the assignment sheet. If necessary, it should be checked daily to insure proper time allotment and provide a basis for checking assignment completion.

The assignment sheet should be numbered sequentially. It should include pertinent information that will also allow for close approximation of grades at any given point. It provides a basis for discussion of study strategies, time management, study habits, and teachers. Provided your child utilizes it properly, it is also a means of tracking progress without the need of progress report circulation. There should be a column with the return date of the assignment and the grade. In this fashion there will be no questions regarding missing assignments. All assignments should be placed in order behind the assignment sheet. If discussions are needed with teachers, the assignment sheet provides a comparison of grades with what has been entered in the roll book. This is very helpful in determining where the system is breaking down and allows for immediate problem solving.

The Art of Perfect Parenting

Organizer - Simply stated, teaching your child to use an organizer is one of the most effective strategies you can use to enhance overall education. Staying organized often means the difference between success and failure.

Privileges tied to performance/GPA - Especially with adolescents, do not be hesitant to correlate the child's activities with performance. There are those who will criticize this as penalizing the child who has tremendous academic difficulties such as learning disabilities. We are very sensitive to this comment. We deal with many such individuals in our office, and in fact, wrote a book entitled "Understanding the Learning Disabled Athlete" (Charles Thomas Pub. 1986). The expectations must be realistic and fall within the child's potential, but the message will be delivered loudly and clearly–THIS FAMILY VALUES EDUCATION.

Bonuses for effort and achievement marks - Sometimes these are more important than the actual academic grade.

Sibling

Many parents are ready to toss in the towel in this category. Don't forget your No Fault Insurance rule.

Fighting

Provoking

Tattling

Intentional trouble-making

Coming full circle with the idea of fairness and role models, many children want to know, as an example, why Mom or Dad can yell, but the kids get a consequence. This is easily remedied, and your child will have a sense of control. Allow your child to give you a "consequence" for the same violation for some of the behaviors. For instance, if it costs them 5 chips for yelling, should you yell, you owe them 5 chips. This also brings inappropriate behaviors to a conscious level on everyone's part.

Definitions

Don't let your ego get in the way of fairness by overruling your child.

I'm certain you feel you can adequately assemble the master plan. Before you do that, may I suggest that you read the last chapter. Not only will it save you much grief in the long run, but many of the stories are quite comical. Kids are really great, but they will test the limits every chance they get. Don't be outwitted.

One area that does not need to be in the contract but certainly needs to be clearly defined for children is that of safety. Children should know: what to do if there is a fire, earthquake, or other disaster; how to turn off the water, power, or gas; how to call for emergency services; what to be aware of with strangers; their own phone number and at least street name; the name of an adult relative or family friend; and anything else that might mean their survival. Don't automatically assume that they will learn all this at school.

Chapter XII - Anecdotes and Pitfalls

May I suggest for those of you whose children can read that you utilize the carbonless telephone message pad from now on. You have a place for the date, time, and message, and, best of all, you have a copy of the exact message. Basic rule of thumb is to put everything in writing. Tape it to your child's mirror, dresser, door, or any other convenient place that he/she will see. This process avoids either the "You never told me about that" excuse or the "That's not what you said" excuse. You can simply pull out your exact message and present it to your legal beagle as exhibit A for the prosecution.

Make sure that everything you set up has a time limit or amount limit to it. Not long ago a young man and his mother came in to the office arguing. She had diligently put together her behavioral contract. The young man insisted that she owed him $11, while she insisted this was absurd. According to the terms of the contract, he could earn 50 cents for emptying the garbage around the house. That was exactly the way it was worded. So this entrepreneurial young man came with his notebook that read, "middle bathroom-tissue-10:58 AM, office trash can-envelope-11:14 AM," etc. He meticulously walked through the entire house every 15 minutes, picked up any trash, even if it were one piece, and logged it in his notebook–22 times before his appointment that day. Needless to say we modified the contract, but much to his delight, Mom had to pay up. She had never placed a limit on this. Keep in mind that many children really get into the contract and look for the loopholes.

Along those same lines, a father and son were verbally sparring just prior to an appointment. When they came in, the father insisted that the son owed him $20 for a curfew violation. The father pointed out that according to the contract, the son had to be in his bedroom by 10 PM. The conversation went something like this.

> "Dad. My contract says I have to be in my room by 10 PM. Right?"

"Right! So what's your point?"

"You came in to have a conversation with me at what time?"

"About 9:50."

"And you left at what time?"

"About 10:15, but what's your point?"

"Dad, I was in my room at 10 PM. You can't fine me."

"Yes, son, but you went out your window at 10:45 PM."

"Dad, show me in my contract where it says that I have to stay in my room. It only says I have to be in my room at 10 PM."

Obviously, this father took the contract home and did some corrections. The son was presented with a 14 page contract at our next session. Maybe a little overkill, but the point got across.

Now, granted that last example was a teenager, but let's try a five and a half year old that I worked with for out of control behavior. We had said in his contract that hitting was a violation that would cause time in his room, and yelling was a regular respect consequence. His mother had brought him to one of his sessions after having hit his teacher. I explained that he knew what the consequences were, and that they applied to school. Tearfully, he acknowledged this and promised he would not do this again. The next day I got an emergency call from his mother. She said that he had hit the teacher again "or something like that." I asked her to bring her son in immediately. That conversation went something like this.

"Dr. Yellen, do I have to go to my room?"

"Let's talk about it. Tell me what happened".

The Art of Perfect Parenting

"You said if I hit my teacher, I would have to go to my room, right?"

"That's right."

"And you said if I only yelled, I would just pay chips, right?"

"Right."

"I didn't hit her!!!"

"What happened?"

"I only pretended to hit her like this (and he proceeded to swing his fist about 18 inches from my face). Do I have to go to my room?"

"Not this time, but if you hit, pretend you are going to hit, throw something to hit, or get someone else to hit, it will count the same as hitting. Okay?"

And I actually did this with a straight face. Of course, inside I'm wondering what law school he will be attending.

Sometimes parents inadvertently set kids up for a fall. One father wanted his son to do well in school. The young man had about a 1.9 GPA the previous semester of high school. Keep in mind that the family was quite well off, so everything is relative. The father told the son that if he pulled straight A's, he would buy him a top of the line stereo system (about $10,000 worth of equipment). But there were no provisions in the contract for what I have previously described as successive approximations toward the goal. The son got three A's, two B's, and one C. This, obviously, was a remarkable improvement from the previous semester, but the young man was left with nothing for his efforts. He reverted back to old behaviors, and we had to work very hard to overcome the damage that was done. Remember that the program needs to be structured for success at all levels. Now I'm sure at this point that you would like to hear a few choice examples that happened with our child rearing. Keep in mind that these are presented with much objection from our son and daughter. They have heard the examples used at seminars, and the thought of finally having these in print did not sit well. But they still have smiles at the idea of what happened.

When my son was just past thirteen, he approached me one Friday evening.

"Dad, could I ask a favor of you?"

"Sure, Josh, what's up?'

"Well, me and the guys want to go to Magic Mountain tomorrow, and I wanted to know if you could drive us there?"

"Sure, no problem. I don't start until about 10 tomorrow morning."

"Thanks, Dad. I'll go call the guys now."

With that he disappeared for about fifteen minutes. He then came back to the room. I knew something was up when he had this half grin on his face and was acting submissive, which is not his nature.

"Hey, Dad."

"Yeah, what's up?"

"Could I ask another favor of you?"

"Ask."

"See, they raised the price. Could I borrow ten bucks for tomorrow?"

"Gee, Josh. I'm really sorry that you don't have enough money, and I hope the next time the guys want to go, you

The Art of Perfect Parenting

have enough. I know you'd have a lot of fun."

"Dad, I already told the guys you would drive."

"Right. No problem because I told you I have the time."

"You're gonna drive them, and I'm not going?"

"No. You can go with me in the car."

The next morning we got up. He followed me around the house without saying a word, figuring I'd give in. We drove all the way out to Magic Mountain, and his friends got out of the car. I looked at him and said, "You need to close the door. We have to get going." In utter disbelief he closed the door and was totally silent. About five minutes from the house he asked, "Have you got anything for me to do to earn money?" The rest of the conversation went like this.

"Do you remember about three weeks ago I asked you if you wanted to clean the garage?"

"Oh, yeah."

"And do you remember how much I offered you?"

"Oh, no. It was $10!!! If I had done it then, I could have gone with the guys today! Can I still do it today, Dad?"

And I, of course, said yes. I know that there are many of you who will say that what I did borders on cruelty. Believe me, it hurt not to see him enjoy time like that with his friends. But as a learning experience, it was necessary. He's never forgotten that lesson and does not "hate" me, as so many parents are afraid of.

The second involves our daughter. When she was about eleven she developed this habit of slamming her door when she was angry. I warned her that if she slammed it again, she would lose it. She came downstairs for breakfast one morning, got angry about something, marched upstairs, and WHAM. I waited until I heard her go into her shower and proceeded upstairs, screwdriver in hand. Quick as a flash, no door. I quickly went downstairs and assumed my proper position at the breakfast table. We all waited. The water went off and about thirty seconds later came this blood curdling scream followed by these intense footsteps coming down the stairs. There before us, with her hair and body wrapped in towels, stood Erit with steam coming out her ears, her eyes wide as saucers, and nostrils flared.

"Where is my door?"

"Hi, Sweetheart. Remember I told you that if you slammed it again, you would lose it? Well, you've lost it for a week."

She proceeded to do a slow burn, turned on her heels, and marched back upstairs. By the way, she has never slammed her door since. I don't consider myself cruel, but I sure wish that I could have taken a picture of her standing there in those towels. Again, a little humor mixed in with a great learning experience.

This last item is an example of allowing children to operate within the boundaries and make choices, even if it is not always the appropriate one. When the kids were somewhat younger, we had this profanity issue. So we made the consequence for profanity $2 per word. There was a period of several days in which the profanity ceased. One morning Heidi and I were down in the kitchen getting breakfast. Our daughter, Erit, came down with this grin on her face. About two minutes later our son appeared at the entrance to the kitchen. If looks could kill, there should have been corpses laying everywhere. He surveyed the situation and proceeded to take two dollars out of his pocket. He looked at us, held up the $2, slammed it on the table, and marched over to his sister. Nose to nose, he loudly shouted, "You a—hole!!!" He then proceeded back upstairs. I calmly went upstairs after him with a very big grin on my face. I stuck my head in his room and just smiled. He smiled, too, and proclaimed, "Dad, it was worth every cent." He knew the consequence and chose to accept it. Had I interfered with the process, I would have negated the entire concept of accountability.

The bottom line is that the loopholes should be tightened up. As stated the program is tremendously effective when handled with consistency. It is time we pass on the values and priorities to our children with love and kindness, yet firmness and structure. We owe them that. Now it's time for you to sit down and get to the details of YOUR contract. Oh, yes. And remember to keep everything in perspective with a good sense of humor.

Chapter XIII - Epilogue

It was always Ma and Pa Cookie's dream to go to Israel during their lifetimes, but one that would go unfulfilled. Our daughter, Erit, was fortunate to go to Israel for six weeks in the summer of 1993. It is customary to place a personal message to God in "The Wall" in Jerusalem. Weakened and frail from his losing battle with cancer, Pa Cookie sent a note with Erit. Normally these notes are kept private, but in this case I'm sure the Good Lord would not mind us sharing the note.

Always the consummate parent and grandparent, even near death, Pa Cookie, in his own hand, wrote

Dear Lord,
please watch over our wonderful grand-daughter Erit Mishelle while she is in our beloved Israel. a special blessing for all of your children and peace and good will all over the world
Shalom
Ruth & al yellen